Sexy CRYPTOGRAMS

Shawn Kennedy

W9-CYA-943

STERLING

New York / London
www.sterlingpublishing.com

STERLING and the distinctive Sterling logo are registered trademarks of
Sterling Publishing Co., Inc.

2 4 6 8 10 9 7 5 3 1

Published by Sterling Publishing Co., Inc.
387 Park Avenue South, New York, NY 10016
© 2008 by Shawn Kennedy
Distributed in Canada by Sterling Publishing
c/o Canadian Manda Group, 165 Dufferin Street
Toronto, Ontario, Canada M6K 3H6
Distributed in the United Kingdom by GMC Distribution Services
Castle Place, 166 High Street, Lewes, East Sussex, England BN7 1XU
Distributed in Australia by Capricorn Link (Australia) Pty. Ltd.
P.O. Box 704, Windsor, NSW 2756, Australia

Sterling ISBN 978-1-4027-5491-3

For information about custom editions, special sales, premium and
corporate purchases, please contact Sterling Special Sales
Department at 800-805-5489 or specialsales@sterlingpublishing.com.

Contents

Introduction

Woody Allen once said, "Sex is the most fun you can have without laughing." Well, consider this book the most fun you can have laughing without sex.

This collection of juicy jokes and titillating tidbits samples a wide range of celebrities from sex symbols, actors, and rock stars—who are all plenty familiar with the subject—to politicians, lawyers, and others you probably wouldn't care to see naked. Along the way, you'll learn Cary Grant's secret to picking up women, Cindy Crawford's favorite body part, and, of course, the status of Woody Allen's sex life—just in case you didn't know it already.

Size matters when solving cryptograms—the fewer the letters, the tougher the solve—so this book is broken into three sections: "Nice and Long," consisting of long, easy puzzles; "Harder, Harder," with puzzles of average difficulty; and "For Sexperts Only," consisting of shorter, more intense puzzles designed to make you break a sweat.

And if you're feeling adventurous, try a "Threesome"—a set of three quotations by the same author. (Each uses a different code.)

Now pull out your pencil, and prepare yourself for the many laughgasms to come!

—Shawn Kennedy

Solving Cryptograms

Are you a first-timer? Don't be shy! These tips and tricks will have you doing it like a pro.

Each sentence is a coded message. The letters of the original message have been replaced with different letters. No letter represents itself, and substitutions remain consistent throughout each individual puzzle. In the example below, each X represents an F, each M a U, each T an N, and so on.

F U N N Y   S E X   Q U O T E
X M T T P   H W V   C M Y A W

Solving relies on trial and error, but these tips will help you break into almost any puzzle:

One-letter words are A or I. Two-letter words are often prepositions such as OF, IT, TO, ON, AS, etc.—one letter is always a vowel. Two-letter words starting with D, G, and T, are DO, GO, and TO, respectively; ones ending with M, P, and R are AM, UP, and OR. O is the only vowel that starts and ends two-letter words.

Words like DID, GOING, NEVER, LITTLE, and PEOPLE have rare letter patterns and are easy to spot. Pattern XYZX is almost always THAT or SAYS. To determine which, see if A appears alone elsewhere in the puzzle. This also helps with pattern XYY, which is often ALL or TOO.

Punctuation contains many clues. Words with apostrophes often end in –N'T, –'S, –'D, –'LL, and –'RE. A two-letter word is I'M or I'D; a three-letter word is often IT'S. A word directly outside quotation marks is often a synonym of SAID or SAYS. If a question mark ends the sentence, the first word is often an interrogative such as IS, DO, DID, CAN, HOW, WHY, or WHAT. If a comma appears after the first word of a sentence, the word before it is probably an adverb and may end in –LY. Try OR, AND, or BUT after a mid-sentence comma, and try AND between the last two items in a series of commas.

Compare short words such as TO and TOO; YOU and YOUR; IT, IN, TO, and INTO; OF, FOR, and FROM; THE, THEN, THEY, and THEIR; and so on.

Note letter frequencies. The most common letters in English are ETAOINSHRDLU, in roughly that order. Letters appearing often are usually vowels, while letters appearing infrequently are usually consonants.

Scan the code for repeated word endings, which are often –ED and –ING, especially in long words or after a doubled letter. Doubled letters are often LL, NN, SS, and TT; try EE or OO in the center of a four-letter word.

Lastly, rule out impossibilities. In XYZ and AZ, XYZ can't be YOU since no common two-letter word ends with U.

If you get stuck, feel around through the sheets and peek at the first word of the answer; that should get you going.

Threesomes

#1

RK PWGQ PUSQ UT CQZZULPQ.
CMQ PFTC CURQ U EFT UDTUOQ F
EWRFD EFT EMQD U GUTUCQO CMQ
TCFCAQ WS PULQZCK.

     —EWWOK FPPQD

LR'Q KAZWLRH OYR KAZORLRH
RGZR BYAORQ. IAR LE RGF
KAZORLRH JPYDQ IFWYT YOBF
FMFPH FLCGR NYORGQ, L TYAWJ
JFELOLRFWH WYYV LORY LR.

XME CMGYMMT B SBT BTH B YFSBT
JBT CM BCXFRVGMRZ YFTHMONVR,
BXXVSPTI ZFV IMG CMGYMMT GLM
OPILG SBT BTH GLM OPILG YFSBT.

#2

J TRAOX FADI OJKY EJICRAI JI

QOO. ORKY EJIC JID SORRX VAPV,

DYH EJIC JID PYDDL CAUZYBD,

PYU EJIC ICYJB EYI IRUZAYD JU

PL YQB.   —YBJTQ FRUZ

WFX CPGF PASPOH VFKFHKFV

SYWFX'H NYHHJR UFBPQHF KCFO

HQHRFBK KCF KEQKC: KCFJE

WFPHQEFWFXKH PEF UFJXN KPDFX

PXV BYWRPEFV.

VTPLJ PKL TGJBP PLH ZGHDPLB IT

V OIJHI, G RVHP PI NI KIZL VHC

BSJLR. VTPLJ PKL TGJBP PRLHPF

ZGHDPLB, G HLQLJ RVHP PI BSJLR

VNVGH VB YIHN VB G YGQL.

U GTUE BP ND EPJBPY BOM PBOMY
ETD, "ND QMCUG UG KSYCUCH."
OM GTUE, "BOTB'G KMJTSGM
GPNMPCM UG BTXIUCH TKPSB UB."
—HTYYD GOTCEXUCH

KETCPVT JVP TBSSKTPO CK
PRWJRLP EKBV TPDBJQ
SPVXKVAJRLP, MBC CWPE OKR'C
OK JRECWZRY XKV AP. AJEMP Z
SBC CWPA KR CKK TKKR.

S GXW'C QXWASGHZ LRAHKJ
VSWVR, PMC XQQFASXWFKKR S
KSVH CX YMC XW F ZXPH FWG
ACFWG SW JZXWC XJ F CHWWSA
PFKK LFQISWH.

#4

SUNKN'Q OCSUXOW LKCOW LXSU
GBZXOW JCTN LXSU SUN JXWUSQ
CO. YPQS DN QPKN SUBS SUN EBK
HCCK XQ EJCQNH.

                    —WNCKWN DPKOQ

EJSSGXAKK? J QYYL WJBCGXG, J
QYYL FGQJB, J QYYL WAJR, JXL J
QYYL HYWJX—YB J VJL HYWJX,
LASAXLGXQ YX EYH WNFE
EJSSGXAKK DYN FJX EJXLRA.

TD'C ZTQQTVKGD LPDDTAL KCPZ
DI DWPCP VWBALTAL DTHPC. T
VBA JPHPHUPJ NWPA DWP BTJ
NBC VGPBA BAZ DWP CPE NBC
ZTJDX.

GR PALQQGLCFQ NJZAH PJYZALCF
NWCV LSRCVWSM CVLC GJBFH,
IZC W SFBFU QLN LSR UFLQJS
CJ AWGWC GRQFAT.

—FGJ YVWAWYQ

RVJ CVP'I WBBYNGMWIN W AVI
WDVJI ZGFVVA, AMXN DNMPE
ZBWPXNC NKNYR CWR DR W
HMCCAN-WENC QVHWP—ZIJTT RVJ
BWR EVVC HVPNR TVY AWINY MP
AMTN.

QJTB HMFLB M ZMTIKGUAUZ PW
CMEU MH YUZ CMBL JHKBLUA PJH
JHZ M CJT IAXTLUZ. TK M TJMZ,
"FUB KEE PU, WKX BCK!"

#6

NX KCVJ NJP NJ GP PYJ ESSZ PYJ

SPYJZ QCLYP CQ G BJWX

QJLICLJJ. DQVSZPDQGPJIX, BYJ

KGB HDBP LJPPCQL YSNJ.

    —ZSEQJX EGQLJZVCJIE

T'A DL DM DOH UQHNH JSSC QDK

LDZHM LQH FBDEH SJ KHG TM AW

BTJH. TM JDEL, T'PH YRKL QDC D

ATNNSN FRL SPHN AW ZTLEQHM

LDIBH.

TS PZJQ'L BQMDCALS ZL WQNNZYW

KZXZRADCAL. NGQ CNGQK XMS

LGQ DCCFQX MN TS RMDQYXMK

MYX PMYNQX NC FYCP PGC TMS

PML.

#7

S JKASG OV VKAZWOAZV S
VSWOVPSXWKLF VITVWOWIWZ PKL
ASVWILTSWOKG, TIW OW WSDZV S
QKW KP OASHOGSWOKG WK ASDZ
OW JKLD.   —DSLQ DLSIV

NLPCP UK QS GQLBTTUPC
MCPBNGCP SQ PBCNL NLBQ B
RPNUKLUKN ZLS DPBCQK RSC B
ZSFBQ'K KLSP BQO LBK NS
PFJCBMP NLP ZLSXP ZSFBQ.

NHG HWTVSIFAL FN XHRFIFZSIH FL
IYSI RFPXN VSLLAI KH ISTRYI
NAAL HLATRY YAU VYFXWPHL
WAL'I VAZH FLIA IYH UAPXW.

HSQ PHSQZ FYXSH Y OGB NGDYFX
KPJQ HP NW OYRQ GFL BSQ DQTH
IZWYFX, "LQQTQZ, LQQTQZ!" BP Y
BHGZHQL VEPHYFX FYQHMBISQ HP
SQZ.   —LQFFYB NYKKQZ

WA BVCR LES V ULS LE LVJGLT
VENXLMMRS DE XUR URLSGDLJS
DC DYJ GRS, LES V'W CVJWMA
ODEZVEORS VX NLZRS WA
MVCR.

TVKDHTA HC SVJZ MUCXHTUKHTA
KV SZ KDUT SN VOT VJAUCS, UTY
TVKDHTA HC PZCC MUCXHTUKHTA
KV SZ KDUT NVLJC.

VH OJLHTEB DZJD MKE YKF'D
UJBBKQ JZHJY, BHJRSFU ZHL
VHZSFY. JFY VH NELH DZJD NZH
YKHNF'D LHJOZ DZH TSFSNZ
VHTKLH MKE YK.   —KRSY

AV QVI COI IVV DITVQB X CNBMI
ZVPO NQIV KVGT YOATVVP. X
BTOXI PXQK IMNQBD XTO
OQMXQZOA YK YONQB DOOQ VQCK
NQ X MXCH-CNBMI.

B XUAT U ODIUL OXD DVVTGP
XTGPTCV HTMUFPT PXT DFWXA AD
ED PD, ULE, MDCE ULE EGS,
AXBLZP DV XTG PTOBLW OXTL
PXT'P IUZBLW CDQT.

Threesomes

SAUT XFP TUTPHX D NKV VDO D
SPMX VPOR, KHC QPMDPLP TP DX
NKV FPMM, VFPPA FPMM, NKDXDHE
XU CU VUTPXFDHE KQUZX DX.

—QPXXP CKLDV

Z VQPMBJQH TIDGVTO VBGWQOTF
TRTFMPSM LFGR Z QGSM VZJPS
SPMBJMGYS GLJTS DZNEV RGFT
VTI JBZS JYG SZETO AGOPTV PS
ATO.

ABK GLA SP FKV, ZOGACPDCTZ GF
CA CF, CF ZSN'F ESHK ST
BIJGTCAD. CA CF EIFA JGT'F
NKFQKOGAK GAAKJQA GA
FIQKOCTAKTNKTLD.

YKNXN LG KFXARD FCDMIAD VKIGN

GNB RLQN, LQ MXIFAOFGY, VIZRA

CIY QLRR YKN VIXRA FY RFXJN

VLYK GZXUXLGN FCA KIXXIX.

     —V. GISNXGNY SFZJKFS

O XOJ XOYYPWC MR GOZW O

GRXW, QNM OVCR QWTONCW GW

ARWCJ'M FOJM MR QW QRMGWYWA

FPMG CWB OJA OVV MGOM CRYM

RH MGPJI.

TYX'I QYJ HLXT LI LXIFMFWILXB

AYP IAF IRWERXLRXW, PAY XFOFM

VYEELIIFT RTJSIFMQ, RMF XYP

FDILXVI?

#12

WYAF JKE IFVUKHYD. OIG VT
KF KOZZFIL JY HF JOWW,
GFHYIOVD, OIG GFAOLJOJVIU,
VJ BVWW HF JKOJ XMSK
FOLVFD.   —XOF BFLJ

SEG QTYY TIN DEV? KAU ONNQ,
KNFNH AHWSNK, SVS? GNYY YNQ'K
OEIPNQ TREVQ QSN KAU ONNQ THX
QTYZ TREVQ QSEKN KNFNH
AHWSNK.

AZK MA PMFZ YPSHMDJ S JSUZ VL
NGMEJZ. ML HVI EVD'B CSWZ S
JVVE YSGBDZG, HVI NZBBZG CSWZ
S JVVE CSDE.

UH CIANSDE CSE S CZSGB SBBSTF
SDE M'U SLGSME M'U BV NPSUZ.
RCMPZ RZ RZGZ USFMDJ PVWZ, M
BVVF BCZ NSJ VLL UH CZSE.

       —XVSD GMWZGA

HPP CD CRXZWJ XRPN CW OHT,
"XZW CHQ YRWT RQ XRS HQN XZW
ORCHQ IQNWJQWHXZ." MRJ XZJWW
DWHJT CD ZITEHQN HQN B TPWSX
RQ EIQL EWNT.

Y SYU LYU BRCCX YFWNUE, UW
ANCBKOWUB YBQCE. TCK HGCU Y
HWSYU SYQCB UOUCKCCU WF
KHCUKT SOBKYQCB, BGC'B Y
KFYSX.

F QCVJKGNOCV TBZDOCFBCGPFD.
F QCVJKGNOCV UBQMPN GJI FC
NPJ OLNJKCBBC. F TOCCBN
QCVJKGNOCV NPJ YBAJ OLLOFK.

—MBKJ AFVOY

CNL UC. CNL GSUJZC TM YMEZC,
FYUKNC TM TMANJC, ETZ CNL
RNYKEUTJP OUANC TM XNETUTO
KM ETPKIUTO UT JUWN GSK
UKCNJW.

H XAF'E MFAL HN CU NHQIE
IWKRVD WKGWQHWFJW LVI
ZWEWQAIWKRVD AQ
ZACAIWKRVD. H LVI EAA
GADHEW EA VIM.

CG THADORP AOYP, "ATBM CQ
GBHK DBBDA," ORP Y TOP EB FHXX
HF CG AZYKE, AB YE MOA EYCQ EB
SQE ETQC PBRQ. —PBXXG FOKEBR

H AL FMNY WHZ OHOD. MJSMCD
FMA OFYV. H'NY IQDFYA OFYV QI,
SFMXBYA OFYV MPLQEA. SFC ELO
VMBY GQE LG OFYV? H'NY VMAY M
GLPOQEY SHOF OFYV.

X EJY ZQR TXWYZ EKUJD ZK HFWD
UL HWJ. XZ ZKKO ZQR TXWR
NRSJWZURDZ TKFW NJLY ZK SFZ
XZ KFZ.

OB ZWICXF IQKJ OX WKK WYQPI
ICX YGFJM WDJ ICX YXXM. ICX
KGWF—G SXDI MIXWJB SGIC W
SQQJVXHAXF PDIGK G SWM ISXDIB-
QDX.   —YQY CQVX

WQJU GDJ FAOZN WQOZNV AZ WQJ
VPDJJZ WQJVJ FGUV WQGW WQJ
LDJZPQ FAZ'W JKJZ BTW AZ
BAVWPGDFV.

BQZZVJSHH VH GQCDBVJT CBS
CSXSMVHVFJ QC OFLI
TVIXNIVSJR'H BFLHS RLIVJT Q
ZFGSI NQVXLIS.

A GBTZ RZBM GB V YVMZ VBY
VJPZY MIZ RGKVB AW JIZ'Y
SEGNFIM VBX LEGMZTMAGB. JIZ
LNHHZY V JRAMTISHVYZ GB KZ.

—JTGMM EGZSZB

YOB SY YSWSFJX ZL JXZ. WLYZ LA
SZ SY QXOZZG CJK, JDK ZNO
XOJFFG RLLK YZMAA SY LMZ LA
GLMX QXSIO XJDRO.

DJCQ LP GO KCW QJI UBPQ
FBFSYCW FCPQLUI LA QJLP
NBSAQWO? CSQBIWBQLNLPU,
JCARP RBDA.

Nice and Long

1. VYO QVY CEL KVY GSUPZ TVIZWO CEUWZ HUTTUYD V BSZJJO DUSW UT TUQBWO YLJ DUPUYD JEZ HUTT JEZ VJJZYJULY UJ GZTZSPZT.

—VWNZSJ ZUYTJZUY

2. ZYDT MZJ FDJFND AWPD NJKD, MYDUD WUD WM NDWRM BJIU FUDRDTM — MYD MZJ WHMIWNNG MYDUD WTX MYD MZJ MYDG'UD MYVTPVTE WQJIM.   —RVEAITX BUDIX

3. FHRJBFK GLDPDFRN ID YLHI XHFXDFRLQRBFK. OHZ XHZSM GZR QF HLKO BF IO HYYBXD QFM B AHZSMF'R SHHU ZG. ADSS, IQOVD HFXD.

—BNQQX QNBIHP

4. KJBGB'F XBGM DCKKDB LYXCZB CR QBR'F QLNLHCRBF OBZLAFB QBR KJCRE, "C ERSV VJLK C'Q YSCRN. WAFK FJSV QB FSQBOSYM RLEBY."

—WBGGM FBCRTBDY

5. BFF VKWZW BTZ ASC VKW
QSYTWCRCB. XZ VKBV CWBFFI B
GCSRFWP XY VKXZ LSEYVCI? PWY
YSV GBIXYH WYSEHK BVVWYVXSY
VS QSPWY'Z RCWBZVZ? —KEHK HCBYV

6. O'JP XRFP LK XRUV XKJOPL
HERVOUT R GKKWPM NGRN NGPV
FKU'N HRV XP OU NGP MPTAERM
CRV RUVXKMP. NGPV EPRJP ON
KU NGP FMPLLPM.

                    —LGOMEPV XRZEROUP

7. VA RDPNA, CW QVYLTDAR GLLO
JVI "RYRTWANDUP WLK VXJVWI
JVUARE AL OULJ VGLKA IRH GKA
JRTR VQTVDE AL VIO." D JVIU'A
VQTVDE AL VIO.   —ETRJ GVTTWCLTR

8. GJXEWTZ JOAVED VX AVXTOXEVJT
WJA XCWSZROI. FOE VR V BZKZ
EBZJED BVEC W TKZWE FGAD, VE'A
FZ WKEVXEVY, EWXEZROI, WJA
UWEKVGEVY.   —XCZIIZD BVJEZKX

9. JTEQANED VFZT ILC YNIT.
ZWTH FYY YLLM FYNMT. NZ'D ELZ
YNMT ZWTH'CT QLEEF VTTZ F
STZZTC-YLLMNEQ JTEQANE DLVTOFH.

—TYYTE OTQTETCTD

10. GZ SJEQ JAWJWXW PA XRMAJAO
PEE XDQ TJODXW SDQA SQ GCUQ
TPNQ. XDCX LPQWA'X ECYQ GQ.
JX'W XDQ DJLJAO XDCX WQQGW
WP KMRQT.

—HPACXDCA UCXY

11. HCAOVR WFPKJFV? QGVR IFGISF
SGGX WFRRFY TORJ RJFOY KSGRJFV
GH, PHA RJF UFT RJPR AGH'R SGGX
WFRRFY RJPH ZGC, VG TJZ WGRJFY?

—IFRFY WCKX

12. EAMSACF FJL BJRL BIR TJGI
JYYICXVM CIJMSVARF SA YJSIK
MAREABF. STIL MJPFI FIGICI
FZIYYVRX. FA ZTJS'F STI SCAPWYI?

—EPFSVR TADDBJR

13. DYUIEMI YUFC. G BGI BUHOE
ZMAHFE QOFAF OF VGAJK MA QOFAF
OF YULFK, XTE OF IFLFA ZMAHFEK
MAGY KFN, IM BGEEFA OMQ XGC UE
UK.   —XGAXGAG XTKO

14. Q PECF AWF PQJFY HFJ AWQJU
NQPP BFA RY QJAE SFL. "ZPFGYF?
Q'PP EJPM YAQIU QA QJ KEV G
HQJRAF." NWGA GH Q, G HQIVENGCF?
                        —SFCFVPM HQIUQJY

15. WP HQYI JFYV WH RV NEMH
VRJZEVD HNIH. JZHP'YH WP WRIJ
HYRDHVRFI TRVH. CFIJ ZQSEVD
JZHW MVHQBHB EI NEMH Q
GFNN-KRBP WQIIQDH.
                        —YHKHUUQ YRWECV

16. HJUJMHFI UILTU XIMX XIJ VLHJ UJY
M VMD IMU, XIJ VLHJ IJ TMDXU. BX
MRUL UILTU XIJ RJUU UJY M VMD IMU,
XIJ VLHJ IJ TMDXU.
                        —FLDMD L'GHBJD

Nice and Long

17. OUG QUC'N CMMQ H AHCFGHFM
BC EUJJUC ZUI YMLGHA IHSSUIN.
HCQ BN PMASY BZ NPM AHCFGHFM
OUG QUC'N GCQMIYNHCQ BY
BNHABHC.   —JHQUCCH

18. NVIUEB AS JGIS WUIKH PUKK,
HXG BUIF UEZGRHGN Q YLVEN LW
KQFUJQ UEHL AS ALVHX. TXGE U
TQFPGN QTQS U XQN HL KYUH UH
QFF LVH.   —FGLEQINL NURQYIUL

19. SLUYU'F HCSLJHD IYCHD IJSL
DCJHD SC KUP IJSL FCVUCHU CG
ECOY CIH FUQ. KU XUYE GYUU IJSL
FUQ — AOFS PYNI SLU MJHU NS
DCNSF.   —UMSCH ACLH

20. GBGXFITX RBGKO-JIIVLK
FIJSGIKG FOG EVYM. J IJTAEVL
KFITPGK FOG GMGBTYK. J RVJQ
VR QNKTX RJBBK VSGI FOG GJIK.
FOG ZVAZ VR FOG VIZJKQ.

                         —JAJTK ATA

21. E V D Y   U N X   S D P Z Z U   B N Y ' Q   Z L O D
P   J X U ,   V D ' Z Z   C D   P Z Z   N F D S   U N X ,
P Y B   P T   T N N Y   P T   U N X   P R Q   Z L O D
U N X   Z L O D   V L I ,   V D ' T   Y N   Z N Y J D S
L Y Q D S D T Q D B .   — C D U N Y R D   O Y N E Z D T

22. V R L Z   A E Z V   K U X X Z M .   B W R O Z
X W Z M Z   U M Z   U   O E X   E C   B U G V   X E
K U S Z   D Z E D O Z   C Z Z O   I E E A ,   R
D Z M V E F U O O G   X W R F S   V R L Z   A E Z V
Z F W U F H Z   X W R F I V .
— D U K Z O U   U F A Z M V E F

23. X G   Z B E R ' G   E J Q   B T T J B H   W P G
G U J   D W Y X D P E   H X S X R C   E U J   G D D S
G D   F J Y D P V X R C   G U J   U B N W P V C J V
G U B G   N B F J   N O   T P H E J   U B N N J V
Z X G U   J Q A X G J N J R G .   — V B O   S V D A

24. Y R F E G ' Z   G R S Y N   E M D   P R B A U T
E V E G   K M R P   K D D Q A U T   T S A Q Y G
E J R S Y   Z Q D D L A U T   V A Y N   Z R P D R U D
Y R   K D D Q A U T   T S A Q Y G   A K   Y N D G
E M D   U R Y .   — P E M T E M D Y   P D E F

Nice and Long

25. WOS WDBNEY UO X ADBEEH
WXJKWRHKVT OSFOZKOVPO RZBG
ADKPD FXZJKPKFXVJW OGOZTO
NVXVSKBNW, ZOAXZYOY, XVY ZOXYH
RBZ GBZO.   —XEOS PBGRBZJ

26. TRF LRQQK YCKHG QEKQ MZ
TRF JRG'Q LCQ MQ XT BMJGMLEQ,
IEKGICU KHC TRF KMG'Q LRGGK
LCQ MQ. KGJ MZ TRF JR, MQ KMG'Q
SRHQE MQ.   —IKUCT UQCGLCY

27. AR LUWDS'R HORRWM PTOR
GUV LU AS RTW CWLMUUH OD QUSF
OD GUV LUS'R LU AR AS RTW
DRMWWRD OSL EMAFTRWS RTW
TUMDWD.
                 —HMD. BORMANJ NOHBCWQQ

28. MZJJHUZA VJO H VDR XZEE.
LWR XKZJ RKZ OVC'P BSZA, PKZ
TBZP KBYZ RB KZA LBCUAHZJO
VJO H TB KBYZ RB V YVTVIHJZ.
                    —OVSHO PDKXHYYZA

29. YUF ASAJD TYU HMD OYAS BNMU
DNMF'LM QYKJZV. DNYD'V MYVF. AD'V
HMDDAUH OYAS BNMU FJZ'LM UJEJSF
DNYD DYRMV VJKM DYOMUD.

—RMXAU EYTJU

30. SV MIORFHF RIO MORZHQAZP,
RJK Q LYHHR FRV: HXOV'NO LYHHOJ
R PYH YA RHHOJHQYJ AYI BXRH'F
IOPRHQNOPV FXYIH FEIOOJ HQSO.

—EQJKV EIRBAYIK

31. P JZWSGU'K HV OZZG LK LU ZYOB.
P'G NYZHLHSB IPUG DBCVSI BVSSPUO,
"JZWSG CZDVHZGB NSVLCV KZWTR DV
IZY ZUTV! KRPC PC DB RZWCV!"

—XZRU HWCR

32. YPJVMSW TLCQBEPY CJSBJIG
RMEXLBE EXP GLOERJYP MG
OYBGEYJEMSW, IMDP YPJVMSW GPZ
CJSBJIG RMEXLBE EXP XJYVRJYP.

—JYEXBY T. TIJYDP

33. M RIFMW RNI'E HIIV SW XUV
ENMJUE CNU KJUMCSBSCT ID VSEWUT,
CNU SFMHSWMCSIW ID VU EMVU,
MWV CNU ECMFSWM ID EUKJUCMJSMC.
                           —XSZZT KJTECMZ

34. N IVS AIM ZKJTNYLNYL V YZY
HQZFS JM WMVFQZR QB. ZYANF N
HVR BNBAMMY N HVR EQTM BVENFNVT
HNAI VBTNXV AIVY EO QHY JQSO.
                           —WQM QTAQY

35. AK QO FJEO UVXZJUZ QAZS
BAKO VX VZSOW IBJXOZD, A QVXYOW
AK ZSOG'BB PO JD VPDODDOY
QAZS ZSOAW VQX HOXAZJBD JD
QO JWO.   —JBPOWZ PWVVED

36. FKN XKTLKNA'Z GAPQWQLQFW
FP RAQWE TFUJRTA QZ AZZAWLQJTTM
J DQCLKNA RALYAAW RAQWE
HFHKTJN JWG IJUQWE ZAC JHHAJT.
                           —ANQXI PNFDD

37. HDT OPDJ, JZ CEDQZ VSXXZEZPKWH DP MZK KBRP JZ VD SP EZRW WSXZ. DP-MZK CEDQSPC SM XRE IDEZ VSMCTMKSPC KBRP EZRW-WSXZ CEDQSPC. —OZWWH ESQR

38. SPYXPBYHSNU HYPWERE EROWHT KREDYRE. DZ SPYXPBYHSNU DE H IYDQR, JNRX JDTT LNRU HYYREL QHGRYE PZ SRYZWQR? —YDINHYK ZTRDEINRY

39. LQU OXMGMLF LJ IOYU GJDU SBMDJGJTRGF MR LQU KQMUS KQOBOKLUBMRLMK PQMKQ NMRLMVCTMRQUR QTIOV XUMVCR SBJI XUORLR. —QUFPJJN XBJTV

40. MT M'E IRJ MIJR H DREHI, M'E FJNHMKLJTRNDHNU. NMKLJ HTJWN FWP M CFCHQQB FHB, "M ZHI'J UR JLMF HIBERNW. JLHIOF TRN ZREMIK RGWN." —GMIZW GHCKLI

41. D YRLNJ LY XF FTYJDAOV JF
VCJVSQFNDXVFMY YVC, TMJ LJ LY
QUHYLADOOH LSQFYYLTOV JF SDRV
OFGV JF D IFSDX IVDNLXP JNFMYVNY.

—UVOVX ODINVXYFX

42. HGOU XDUUQDER QT QL ZUGOCBR
QN HGOU IQNR TDHT, "HGO'UR GLBH
QLZRURTZRS QL GLR ZJQLE," DLS
HGO MDL'Z URXRXCRU IJDZ QZ QT.

—XQBZGL CRUBR

43. H SAIVNY I EHUQ FDC ONIUV
CWQO FC YHVSCTNU FAIF ANU
FIVFNV DNUN NMISFQO QHGN RHWN:
DN DNUN LCFA SUIBO ILCKF EHUQV.

—EUCKSAC RIUM

44. WJ GJLVCOK DQYS HEJ'M
ZEJACZM BEY OERENS. KWVB EB
MKGN REJ'M PGVCGAG CM ZWJ PG
REJG, WJR MKG EMKGY KWVB WYG
RECJL CM.   —HCJOMEJ ZKQYZKCVV

45. RLAY FP BZY TYRFMZBUSR
FHBYGAIR OYBXYYH CYYBFHM I
OYISBFUSR MFGR IHT TFPKLAYGFHM
BZIB PZY RLLNP RFNY I ZITTLKN.

—WLZH OIGGDCLGY

46. GV QI PCV IRL CTSV JQ EQGVZ
PQ TKP LJ KTHVH QI QZTM-BVJLPTM
LJPLYTKD, NJMVHH LP LJ HQYV GTD
QRHPZNKPH LJPVZHPTPV KQYYVZKV.

—U. VWBTZ CQQSVZ

47. UIF USVF UFTU PG QPSOPHSBQIZ:
HFU UXFMWF NFO UP SFBE UIF
CPPL BOE BTL JG UIFZ HPU BO
FSFDUJPO. JG NPTU TBZ ZFT, JU'T
QPSOPHSBQIJD. —X.I. BVEFO

48. YE FZJ EG DB ZXIYEEBX EFZE UB
BHAOYJF FZMB JBQ GH EFB DKZYH,
UFYVF YJ Z MBKW CHJZEYJSZVEGKW
ROZVB EG FZMB YE.

—IZOVGOI ICAABKYXAB

49. NF EHFURZXZKTHW WZXO ND
WRMW M XZW ZL NDY HSLLDI LIZN
EIDNMWSID DGMUSXMWTZY, QSW
WRMW'H YZW WISD. VZNDY HSLLDI.

       —IZQDIW HURTNNDX

50. BI KJM'YW WCWY BV PJMUO TA
OJ SLWOLWY KJM ALJMNP EBAA T
DMOW ZBYN, TNSTKA ZBCW LWY
OLW UWVWIBO JI OLW PJMUO.

       —OLJQTA DTYNKNW

51. JQX MBNS JTMYHNX RGJQ
CXZYDNNS NGHXTDJGBL RMWXB
GC JQDJ JQXTX DTXB'J XBMYLQ
CXZYDNNS NGHXTDJXA WXB JM LM
DTMYBA.   —LNMTGD CJXGBXW

52. E NIUORL OK MR REODRP I
JEIUK JAITRP EU I NDKPRDKXCR
KP I JKAEOEZEIU. IUL OK ORAA
ODR OPXOD, ODRPR ECU'O HXZD
LEYYRPRUZR.   —DIPPT C. OPXHIU

53. NDQ GN V MFSZDKNVRGFS MVKKGDJ FHR OT FRYDK BDVSN. GE TFH PDR FS UDII FHR FE ODJ, YVIE RYD XKFOIDBN FE ODJ VKD NFIZDJ.

—XDRDK HNRGSFZ

54. MHC DHUPY, XEP JPZX VGECHITZTVRZ VCP DHCIZ. XEP S-ZGHX TZ TY XEP PVCZ. EP DEH WHHBZ MHC TX JPWHD XEPCP TZ DVZXTYS ETZ XTUP. —TZVJPW VWWPYIP

55. XCTIJPCSN WI BWNJ VUZ IJL. JKJSE AWOJ W ZC WA W IPJUS W PWBB HJKJS ZC WA UDUWH. THAWB AXJ HJLA AWOJ YCOQUHE YCOJI.

—OUSWBEH ICNCB

56. UV ZXYBTFJP JAFKR FK JAP QBTMG FH X WBN BZ ZFKP PCTBOPXK DABDBMXJPH, QAFDA FH GPZFKFJPMV UCDA WPJJPT JAXK HPN.

—XMFDFX HFMYPTHJBKP

Nice and Long

57. H KPHAW FNF QMRHG PYR
LCDNJMKHNAHOCX NLYJ
HAKCLGNMLRC QNLC KPYA YAVKPHAZ
CJRC KPYK PYR CDCL PYFFCACX, YAX
DHGC DCLRY.   —TLYAW OYFFY

58. EGCZW KVZ ARZ OAVGWIZOA
CKIWZAO XW ARZ JWXBZVOZ; CZW
KVZ OXCTDH QRZKT CZAKD. KWF EZ
QKW KDD KIVZZ ERZVZ WGVAR XO.
                —DKVVH CXDDZV

59. D KTNF EB DO WZN MDHWDNM.
IRET ZLDT ZLX WR VN MWTLDKZW
LOX IRE ZLX WR VN MUDOOI LOX
ZLJN OR VRRVM. DW FLM QDUN ORW
SI NTL.   —VNTOLXNWWN BNWNTM

60. KMDOA LMDYSXZA XQMNG POF
DMIO MCGOA GTXA DOA. GTOZI
JIZYOP CXSS ZAGM GKM DXEMI
LXGOJMIZOP: AMG OAMNJT, XAB
GMM DNLT.   —XAA SXABOIP

61. RZD QMUIGLWQDZX MU XJBX
XR TD B WRRL ARHDC, XJD WGK
QGUX JBHD B JGQRZWRGU VDZMU
BZL BZ DCDNXMRZ KRG NBZ UXCMYD
QBXNJDU RZ. —UGD IRJBZURZ

62. R ODY RG JITFNJ DGX ZJKDG QF
WDMM RG MFBJ ORQU DCJTRHDGY RG
IGRWFTC. DGX R HFGQRGIJ QF UDBJ
QUDQ MFBJ DWWDRT.
—CDXJMJRGJ DMZTRKUQ

63. NP HERDMIXMPXM, VRUPRTUHVJW
NI H IAKIZNZAZM SRU IMC, YJMUMHI
NP HEADZJRRE IMC NI H IAKIZNZAZM
SRU VRUPRTUHVJW. —MELAPE YJNZM

64. PFW NZONHPNLW EK QWYHL
TWDYQNPW YR PFNP UFWH SEC
RWW N IGWPPS LYGD, SEC HWWZ
HEP LGYWOW EOWG FNOYHL NH
CLDS EHW NP FEJW.
—INCD DWNCPNCZ

65. KEKLUOMTW, DGS GQEKO CKIS
GKB DKXSO SOAQMG DUES PCAE
DGUOXUOM KZAQD PAAJ AC BSV DA
ICSKDS KTT DGS KCDB KOJ BIUSOISB.

—EKBAO IAATSW

66. CPGO IGO HSXO HPTXHGGO VOM
FSMMGOAB XGVKP ZSRGXHB, HPGB
HPTON HPGB ATNG CJIGO. VKHSVAAB,
BJS'XG YSFH PJXOB.

—YSAGF UGTUUGX

67. JI ZVFK IY DF EYZ'K DF
FBDWNNWVVFK IY CFI QYAKYBV,
DZI DZEJAC QJCWNFIIFV LWV YUWE.
AYL JI'V IOF YIOFN LWE WNYZAK.

—RWQUJF BWVYA

68. AB GRVB R LPRI RY OSNXXP YX
GBBY QI NBM HRMRHB RIV WQOO.
QY ARO PQWB R PQYYPB UZOQIBOO
VBRP. Q WQOOBV NBM YNBI Q MRI
NXGB.

—UMRV LQYY

69. XLS QGWQLWPADPLX GW
JRDP'X GW PRL GEPXHNL GC PRL
HWNHTHNEDI. HP'X CEWWZ OLQDEXL
H PRHWY HP'X OLPPLA GW PRL
HWXHNL. —DILS JDIXR

70. VTZEKY PCP RJKHTRH OLQEKY
QJLYU GPI EG QJLYUXC PSLEWTXPKH
HJ HQCEKY HJ QPTO OJGHJCPWGZC
JK T QJXXPQ RJTGHPQ.
—APKKT ATVPGJK

71. STC EOIFS QOFF OF XZDOP,
STC FCPNMR OMSOXZSC, STC STOIR
INVSOMC. ZESCI STZS JNV UVFS
SZQC STC DOIK'F PKNSTCF NEE.
—IZJXNMR PTZMRKCI

72. ZBICXCMU CV, LPWBZ VBH, WKB
VBFMUE MIEBVW ZBVMYZFB SKCFK
KYJLU TBCUXV KLNB LNLCILTIB WM
WKBJ PMZ TIMSCUX WKBCZ JCUEV.
—VYVLU VMUWLX

Nice and Long

73. AR JFFJU TXHX JQPPXH DCNK
NYY AR VHQXKLU' NKL Q TNU NVHNQL
DF UCFT DCXA. KFT Q SZUD VXXY
DCXR'HX YQIX NK NWWXUUFHR.

—SXUUQWN UQABUFK

74. GIQ BML'F WPCPCUPW TPO. GIQ
BML WPCPCUPW FZP KMBF IK YF,
WPBMNN VZPWP YF VMT MLA FZP
APFMYNT, UQF FZP TPO BMLLIF UP
WPCPCUPWPA.   —P.N. AIBFIWIV

75. PNT AQVN GL QBIGHNE QTE
AIPNT SMWTV, "MIA OQT MN AQTS
PN AMNT W FIIV SMWH AQU?"
SMNBN'H TI ZFIIE QTUAMNBN TNQB
IGB ILSWO TNBJN.   —QTEU BIITNU

76. TMVHPZVHT NMY UHQGGN JZD Q
DZUG PCH VMVHRP NMY OZTT CHU
AYP PCHR NMY DHP JZTPUQLPHJ AN
PCZRDT GZOH CHU MGJHU TZTPHU.

—EMCR THAQTPZQR

77. O'N OA YTQFX FY KTVVOAI GMZ
GFNMEUOAI MVGM, TAC OE GUFJVC
OAKVJCM MQMXREUOAI YXFN
POGGOAI EF GOEEOAI KVFGM
EFIMEUMX.   —GUMXM UOEM

78. P XOW'U JKJW RPWV ELNJLWJ
RLG O YBOULWPX GJBOUPLWESPY,
NZXS BJEE USJ IPWV DSJGJ ELNJLWJ
DOWUE UL EJJ NJ WOIJV.
                    —TPBMJGU TLUURGPJV

79. N FBHTUWB YNJ QA YBNJ DZ
DWYBXT OBDORB'T ZNSBJ HDJUBT.
HGW WYB XBNR TYDES FNT WYNW
QA HDJA UT QGEY ZUEBX.
                    —ZUEDRRBWWB TYBXUJNZ

80. NZTVT'Q QDETNZUKM GTVP
QTWP XSDON STUKM QOSEUQQUGT.
PDOV MOXVR UQ RDLK, QD PDO ZXGT
ND NDNXJJP QOVVTKRTV PDOVQTJB.
                    —TGX JDKMDVUX

81. BJ YGXYOOYJV PYUDZJ PIZEOR
AY OMSY B PSMUV: PIZUV YJZETI
VZ BUZEPY MJVYUYPV AEV OZJT
YJZETI VZ XZWYU VIY YPPYJVMBOP.

—UZJBOR SJZG

82. SCV TWRH Z DZJ ZHHMDR Z XEIB
SCW GBEIOH SZJOH CED OW QEHH
CRI? JEJR OEDRH WMO WG ORJ, HCR
WJBV SZJOH CED OW SZJO OW QEHH
CRI. —CRBRJ IWSBZJT

83. IQGIRQ DUCXV C KRQQI YCDU
QJQWFGXQ, NZD C'S XGD RCVQ DUED.
C RCVQ VCKKCXO, NZD DUED'K ERR.
C'S XGD UEJCXO KQB MGW E FQEW.

—IEWCK UCRDGX

84. ZMCJ QCJ MSDC QLJCE SJH
YLZCB AMCE UCA AXBJCH LJ
PCKXSIIE. AMCE UCA MLBJE SP
MCII. O FSJ'A OQSUOJC ZME,
AMLXUM. —YCJCILYC PYMCCBOP

85. UM UYTDUGWIWAZLN ZL NDG
FGLN DJLFUMQ UMC XWKUM TUM
DUBG; NDG WIQGY LDG AGNL, NDG
KWYG ZMNGYGLNGQ DG ZL ZM DGY.

—UAUNDU TDYZLNZG

86. QFPQMF XIP TBZ HSBUVJUPVT
TFY JT OP TVCTUJUVUF GPS
HSBUVJUPVT WJPMFODF PCWJPVTMZ
IBWFO'U IBE FOPVHI HSBUVJUPVT
TFY. —HFPGG TQFBS

Harder, Harder

87. "F" QAZCX BWA WAUP FABX BWA
FSUD. "U" QAZCX BWA TSDDZSC FABX
BWA FSUD. JHB "K" QAZCX ATAUGJPRG
FABX BWA FSUD.   —NSUN RPHFDZX

88. UTOK NOMNCO JDE, "EMV'IO
WIODASKB FE TODIY," YTOE VJVDCCE
LVJY FODK YTDY EMV'IO WIODASKB
YTOSI BOKSYDCJ. —LOQQIOE WOIKDIG

89. H ZHIINM UK LHGIR SHGJ WOM
IUQZNM UK LHGIR XHSWGNRRN
QO RDN IWUN MWK. H DWFNO'R
DWM RHUN LQG RQCWXXQ IHOXN.
                —WGRYGQ RQIXWOHOH

90. ARV YMJR LVTF XEL ZRRTCVKU:
YPVKNF MVW YLNVF. C XRTT AF
ECZR, "CZ C WLV'X YMJR MV
RNRSXCLV, AMHR AR M UMVWECSY."
                —QLQQF UTMFXLV

91. B PZEY XDO PXD PXBJN B EZADY
WZHP VRZFP XDO GVH XDO WBJY.
PXVP'H GXVP B PZEY XDO PZ NDP
BJPZ RDY GBPX WD JVCDY.

—HPDADJ GOBNXP

92. X'JZ LCDQ YAGZ QFNACYF DA PCBF
XG PT IXKZ QFVQ OCIIXGY PT QAO CO
LCDQ SAZDG'Q DZZP IXEZ QFVQ HXY
AK V SZVI.

—GXBAIZ NXBFXZ

93. HTMFUP RI YMRI ZQYRFUYGFSU,
GKZI YCWZH RZ FL F EYC
KSRSCZQTYA. F CYFH F EYCU'G
NTG F EYC EFAAFUP GS AZYMU.

—NFAA RTMMYI

94. EGO ZPISWOB VK, UIM
OTHVZZOM HK DVEG C ZOYVK CYM
C SPCVY, SHE YIE OYIHUG SWIIM
EI HKO SIEG CE EGO KCBO EVBO.

—PISVY DVWWVCBK

Harder, Harder

95. JIPTGIT PJ STQL JPXPNUQ RC
JTZ. JCXTRPXTJ JCXTRWPGM BJTABN
ICXTJ CA PR, HBR RWUR'J GCR RWT
QTUJCG ET'QT FCPGM PR.

—QPIWUQF ATLGXUG

96. NY QIZZVNYR SOWWUZ, GBH
YZZV THFW BYZ QHUU DBI ZAZIG
WPZYWG-DNAZ SBPF. HYUZFF WKZ
SBPF OIZ MYBPY FUHWF.

—TBKYYG SOIFBY

97. D'W IDOA Z WAYJ ZQ Z CAZIIT
ALXAYFDRA CAFQZJCZYQ. TBJ UZY
IBBO ZQ WA ZII TBJ XIAZFA, GJQ
TBJ UZY'Q ZSSBCH WA.

—ZYYZ OBJCYDOBRZ

98. UR BJX PJQMUWLF GLSFUQN S
CXMY-XC HFS DJ SQ SXWUDUJQ
ESQUCXKSDUJQ, DYLQ BLM, U
PJXKW HL PSKKLW S ESQUCXKSDJF.

—SKBMMS EUKSQJ

99. E JPEOS EJ'M YAKDJ JECZ LZ FKJZT
QKH MZOYJKHM LEJP AHZYMJM. YQJZH
YNN, LZ'FZ AZZO ZNZBJEOV AKKAM
NKOV ZOKDVP.

—BNYEHZ MYHVZOJ

100. YUN IFWQL NV XOV PYXP NV
WXA OVXWY UFO BVARPXIK
RAKPVXZ UH PYXP KDUP UA UFO
MXWQ PYXP RPWYVK.

—HIXKY OUKVAMVOB

101. MRKDKFKX MYZKD GCJIQPRJ,
CAA JRK TYWU CXK UKGXKJAW
RYSQDP QJ MQAA KFKDJHCAAW
JHXD QDJY UKN.   —WCUZQDK TAKKJR

102. Y JCTD OU YVVNAYUOA UL PDYOR
C ADB AGFPUV. Y MUO'S JCTD QCXIA
UL EUFDO XJCAYOR FD MUEO SJD
ASWDDS VYID PWCM QYSS UW
AUFDUOD.   —SUPDG FCRNYWD

Harder, Harder

103. SO S YNHN WUM, S'C KXNND
YSBA XNRZUHCR CSLUDHSR. FVB
RZXM ORH BAN XRZW AUSH AN AUC
SZ "BAN IUZ SZ BAN SHRZ IUKQ."

—FNZ UOOXNLQ

104. IETQM MEO DLL YBHJD TEBXY
EX ISL DFHLLX ASQI ISLM ODLT IE TE
EVV ISL DFHLLX IE YLI EX ISL DFHLLX.

—YLXL QOIHM

105. PR KXOCUZT OUQT VS PL, "Q
EUZ'V ILPLPCLI JKLZ JL WUOV KUT
OLH," UZT Q OUQT, "JLWW Q EUZ
UZT VKUV'O JKR JL UQZ'V TSQZF QV."

—ISOLUZZL CUII

106. UWVM TPYD'G TGGPTFGYN
GC IY RYFTWMY CO IV IBDN.
GQYV'PY TGGPTFGYN GC IY
RYFTWMY CO LQTG B NCD'G IBDN.

—UVJMV PCMY XYY

107. ZSA EAPZ PAK ANTRDZWXH
YXM FWNP WP CSAH NDNNQ BDZP
LXLLQ XH ZSA YDHHQ CSAH SA
RXLAP SXLA YMXL CXMF.

                    —CWGGWDL S. LDPZAMP

108. FCO TF IYCNACFA PECH TA'F
MTJC GNFJCAGNMM: BHC-BH-BHC
PTAE NF MTAAMC XYTGGMTHI NF
VBFFTGMC.   —MCFMTC HTCMFCH

109. HJZ NZOH XWLH WNPGH NZABR
AB W LZDWHAPBOJAX AO JWQABR
OPSZNPKV LARJH HJZLZ HP KP AH
TAHJ TJZB VPG'LZ JPLBV.

                    —FZBBV SUUWLHJV

110. FLA KWYOR VOLLX KENU M
PEQDQOL XHWIEREAS EN UMR NUL
HESUN QWOWH OEX SOWVV WA.
NULD UMIL AW VUMFL.

                    —NWHE MFWV

111. K A Y F T U Y K U K T S I C F J Y F D F
U Z W U U Z F M B Y O W B P C Y S J S L Y A W J
R G T A U Y S T S R C B F W K U K Y K U S O W Q F
O W J F K K U G M Y H.   —H W D F C W B B P

112. O Z F P I L N B F D J O L O B R H O R
K O E I : B R I O H L B G U O R M I P I U Q V W J
G U Q, L Z I B L Z I U O H L B H K I I V N O L Z
I P I U Q N B D F R B R I F U L Z. —B K O P I U U I I G

113. U E Q X Q P W J X A N R N F Z I A
W Q I W P U P C Q E Q U Q X A W Q B M R F R F P C Q
O E A P W I' U J X Q A L L M J P Q G O P U E E P W
F R U Q I U E A H A W Q B M R F P U Z.
                    —I A X H R I H R P F Q X

114. E H E N C E' O E A D G A U G O I Q F G
Z G R A N. U C G W C R D G G J S M G N N E Y A,
V Y O G N U W, N G J R S S G R Q,
N E V S Q E P E U W — R Q Q E H R A U E A
V W P Q Y U C G N.
                —W D G N N R E A U Q R F M G A U

115. TS T'Y PFY FD QFVL
IZAR FSSFTHD FD T'AR ORRV
BHRYTURY SZH, T'Y OR TV F
MFH FU PFHAFHY QRYTBFI DBPZZI.

— SHFVX DTVFUHF

116. TDHVK UTBVQ CKV OPV WVNO
CO BCIAQF DTYV: OPVS CDUCSN
OPAQI OPVS BCS WV HTAQF AO
ZTK OPV DCNO OABV.

— ACQ ZDVBAQF

117. DPR KRXD FJE DS XWGGRRV
FNDP DPR SZZSXNDR XRU NX KE
DRCCNIQ PRY ESW'YR NBZSDRID.
XPR GJI'D FJND DS VNXZYSTR ND.

— GJYE QYJID

118. TLEY ILMNLET ZDY EZNY LQ
TPYYO WMBYTBWMYT, UYB W VZT TL
TIZDYN BPY QWDTB BWEY W VLDY
BPY VPLCY TPYYO.

— NZMMU VWCCWZET

119. QVGIG JXK LG JXDK QVCDAY
LGQQGI QVXD YGZ, XDH YPJG
QVCDAY JXK LG BPIYG. LMQ
QVGIG'Y DPQVCDA GZXNQOK
OCTG CQ. —B.N. RCGOHY

120. OVJVHHVP RQ YUORVYUS
JKUO-VTO CUI. RO'Q GKRYW
QEVYQVHKC GI XKWKOUHRUYQ,
YVO KDMRGRORVYRQOQ.
—CUXRC SKOOKHJUY

121. PFRIY SK UYJ PNFCCYIU ZGC'S
YJEFCZ GWO NGOTVGCU, ZGC'S
DFXY WU RYSSYO EYGEIY, FCZ
ZGC'S PGDY TC PIYFOIM YCGWLN.
—RTII DFNYO

122. M IHF'X ZJOZBR OTZK VFITKOTZK,
TRLTWMZJJB MF XNT NTZX. MS M'U
OTZKMFD Z SJHOTK IKTRR, ONB IH
M FTTI VFITKOTZK?
—FZHUM WZULCTJJ

123. C'AD GDADI PBK JR EIDJDGK JR LD PBACGU NDQ XCJP BGMRGD. C UODNN C'Y TONJ VODDG RH JPD HRIDEFBM KCNNRFAD.

—TOFCB IRLDIJN

124. ZLQO SM DEL GSBNDOM IBP TSTDA-DEL MOJLBPM LT MKNSMUSBW BLSMOM DUID MULEM ALNF GSBP SMB'D JZSJYSBW FSWUD.

—HLUBBA FLDDOB

125. K SJFF JF K QPNAQT OXJRS HAFJIVAH UT VKOGXA OP FOPE FEAARY ZYAV ZPXHF UARPDA FGEAXCQGPGF.

—JVIXJH UAXIDKV

126. FMYUDMN IEFD HCIJQJFDF UQW PQWCYQCUDN JF U REIUQ AEQVJQV DE GC U FCO EGXCMD. DNUD'F XPFD QED UAA FNC RUQDF DE GC.

—GCDDZ YEAAJQ

Harder, Harder

127. L F J P V Q L O J K F D A C Q L O , Q J O V F P
Q X F J Q C M O X , C M F C C M O P C M Q Y N M C
D C V F K K O T , J Q C P Q Y C M , C M F C ' K
V F K C O A Q J C M O P Q Y J N .

—H F J O C M F X X D K

128. F Q O R G Q B B Z F C Q A D H
W P Q J E J X F E I E G ? J S K E O H S D Y
C Q A B S P S E B Q I E G , H Z S B Q O X A
Z E N S I E A S H W S P I M E H M S X D R S
K Z Q K Q X E M S .   —K E P P D S H G Q B

129. R X S K X N W O M R B J P I B P M D Y G B
N H K B Q L U N F J X B Z N Z B ? Y L X B
I H N R K P H S J X Y H T P V N W J Y J , X B
K X N W O M H ' J !

—T B N U T B V B U H P U M K X P R

130. N R T F ' E H Q E O J L T G J E O N F Y
J B J X I F N Y O E , E O J L T G J Y J L E A X J L .
E O T E ' H W J K N V J S A E E N F Y Q F H N X E I
S T F E N J L J B J X I H T I .

—W X N Y N E E J W T X H Q E

57

131. ZFNHN'C TUZFRTD YNZZNH
ZFKT DUUE CNS. YMZ YKE CNS? K
JNKTMZ YMZZNH KTE INOOL CKTEXRAF
RC YNZZNH ZFKT YKE CNS.

—YROOL IUNO

132. TLBV IJO'UB S FDUP TDEL NDF
NUBSAEA SVK S FUBSE LJE NJKI TDEL
ADH TJZBV TLJ SUBV'E, IJO YJOPK
ASI ELSE'A S LSVKDYSR.

—MBCC RUJNAE

133. BT J HSPX PMEFS BOE PMEFS
BOE UPUUFS UPXBSE UIF UPNC,
J GJOE UIBU J DBSF MFTT BOE
MFTT XIP HPFT UP CFE XJUI XIPN.

—EPSPUIZ M. TBZFST

134. WE KYA NGA WDCMDAMA EYT
MLMTRQYAR CY NGLM KTYFU XMO,
W KFMXX NM'A NGLM KWLMD FX
GSS JYTM YTKGDX.

—JGSPYSJ QTGAQFTR

Harder, Harder

135. XGW XMCPIVW JSXG AWFOCMO SO
XGNX XGWU JCMMU SZ N BSMV GNO
AVWNLNBW. XGWU CPBGX XC JCMMU
SZ OGW GNOF'X NFU.

—QNMSVUF QCFMCW

136. ALMXN UME PU YHCTMLGVS
YBPSM PN'U BXZZMCPCA, WVN YBH
LMJMJWMLU ALMXN UME NBMK BXT
PC CPCMNMMC MPABNK-NBLMM?

—WHW UMAML

137. S GZQE S VRN S CQZ'I VBJJH
ESIF LRPPSJC LJZ, KAI EFRI S
LJRZ SV IFRI S CQZ'I VBJJH ESIF
FRHHSBN LRPPSJC LJZ.

—KPSII JGBAZC

138. ARINWFQRNHYM HI MYNPHMZ
NY QU RIPRAUG YX, QWN HN'I
MYNPHMZ NY QU KRFNHOWERFEL
KFYWG YX UHNPUF.

—ARNN ZFYUMHMZ

139. PNA JLLNJQ SP YSYZE
LNOGNRZ VTJZ EMI'UN XMZ JRC
YSYZE LNOGNRZ VTJZ LNMLQN
ZTSRF EMI'UN XMZ.

—PMLTSJ QMONR

140. PIGSG KWY W FZSR DQAHDZQF AQ
BE IAPGR SAAB VAAS WRR QZFIP
RWYP QZFIP. Z JZQWRRE IWV PA RGP
IGS ALP AJ BE SAAB.

—IGQQE EALQFBWQ

141. YJQLX D GJA GFZYWO NDG VW PW
IQVN DL DVVQVSPJ, LWV OWWCG.
ZWGV ZJL VNQLC QV'G OWWCG;
IWZJL CLWI WVNJHIQGJ.

—CDVNOJJL VSHLJH

142. DSZDES JBZ EPUS PL TEMHH
BZWHSH HBZWEO RMIS HWAS KZ
DWEE KBS YEPLOH JBPES ASRZUPLT
KBSPA KAZWHSAH.

—HDPIS RPEEPTML

143. TEHFMGTEQQ PH GOM HMUXIW
RXHG MCUPGPIV PIWXXS HAXSG,
EIW GOM XGOMS XIM HOXYQWI'G
OEZM HAMUGEGXSH.

—WPUF ZMSGQMPT

144. UNO? WBKFXMWBJMNCI, JU IFW
QNM FCLNX, MVNXN JXN FMVNX
MVTBQU MVJM ENGFPN PFXN
TPDFXMJBM TB IFWX LJTCI CTKN.

—JCNO MXNENA

145. L JMTQQCR VCMMLXV MEC VLSU
KPTIM MCX BCKSJ KVT, AELOE LJ
WIJM KJ ACUU PCOKIJC L'R
GTSVTMMCX AEKM L AKXMCR ECS
GTS.   —WTEX AKBXC

146. VNMQM PH BSCE BSM
QMTWQO VB UNPAN VNMQM PH
SB WSHUMQ: "UNWV WQM EBD
IBPSK UPVN TE UPLM?"

—TPKDMC IM AMQFWSVMH

147. QJBKKPVU PQ WZAAZL AJGV QZE.
PN XBY'LZ VBA QGAPQNPZC, XBY RGV
TGOZ GV ZERJGVUZ NBL QBTZAJPVU
XBY LZGDDX DPOZ.

—GCLPZVVZ UYQBNN

148. LFQMK IKDPNDWQJV NJOURVK Q
RW WRYQJV MNXK UN ULKJUH-PQXK
UFNZORJC IKNIMK. RJC UFKJ Q VN
FNWK RMNJK.   —ARJQO ANIMQJ

149. UB BUX GU NYXGK KGIYN QGUP
ZBJHP WCHH QX C UTQOYBQCUGCW.
CANXK CHH, G BUHT VHXXO ZGNY
IBBP-HBBMGUI QXU.

—AGBUC OGNN-MXNYHXT

150. ZKQJ HASU GU HIMX OMKDQ,
XPUQN WAP, WVL W DUWKJAXKM
RWPJVUP — WVL TIK OWV EUUR JNU
HIMX OMKDQ WVL XPUQN WAP.

—ZWOE DUVVT

151. T LPVQE IBAK KVA SLPA IDS TUSD
QDMC VUE QDRR SD NTMC BN YDZPU.
T ETEU'S IPS TUSD QDMC SD NTMC BN
YDZPU, OBS T KBQP VEVNSPE.

—SPE UBIPUS

152. VKKQTFK WSMR ILS LTYK RKA ICVL
VLKCJ LSV WPSQXK VKTZLKJR TJKQ'V
XTOTFKX GCXR. VLKM'JK PDZGM
WTRVTJXR. —FKSJFK ZTJPCQ

153. IGNUJ NZMXF VU WCTCVBU
GK KCDZJM GYMCEN, VAF GJBH
NUJ CYU WCTCVBU GK KCDZJM
IXGBU YUBCFZGJEXZTE.

—EXCYGJ EFGJU

154. PNZ JZXAZP PQ DQVB DLOZ LJ
GQBH, INGJLXHD ZCZAXLJZ, ZHPLVB
KZDD, HVT JZC. DQPJ QO JZC. HJ
YEXN JZC HJ GQE XHV BZP.

—XGVTL DHEIZA

155. C TMNN PCJ OQ C PIKKC, C
HRQNYMIJ KCAT, IA CJ QUPSCKCYMIJ
GIMJY. YZCY'N OCNMP NGQSSMJD
CSS EIKQJ IRDZY YI TJIE.

—KMNYMJDRQYY

156. RXID I SIV GVHBPZ IEBLD
I RBSIV'Z MUBDXGZ IWG XTZ
QIVDIZTGZ BQ XBR ZXG RBLUN
UBBO RTDXBLD DXGS.

—EWGVNIV QWIVMTZ

157. HXB HBJKG XMFN NFND CXBJAXC
IBJ TBJKG GSN ODBR LNZ? SC HML
RJTX RBDN OJU HXNU IBJ WJLC HNUC
CB XNKK.   —WBXU HMCNDL

158. VC V JTAT YIMTQ CHA Y HZT-KVZT
YZIJTA EH "JRYE OYMTI Y JHOYZ
XHHQ VZ DTQ?" V JHGKQ IYL, "Y OYZ
JRH VI XHHQ VZ DTQ."

—DHD XGWWVHZT

159. CTJ IXUC OKBXP H TXR UJA
OHCT XNUKIECJIF TXCJR BJ. H
VKEIR CJII NF CTJ OXF UTJ XUZJR
SKY CTJ BKPJF.   —RYJO VXYJF

160. GU JMCU DUMINQ VN
FUARUCU VJMV EMQ YRDIV
GMALUZ OWDRHJV VN YDUU JRI
JMQZI YND EMIVODFMVRNQ.
                    —ARAS VNEARQ

161. C GOROZO OL BPLD WORI C
GCTGIU-XOTI SIZJI. OD HCZCKIL DY
VTYDIJD DNI VTYVITDE XODNYPD
YGLDTPJDOZK DNI QOIX.
                    —BYIE CUCHL

162. CKBGKA YEG ACSZ SEOAA
HACFZ C ICB ZEGDFI DKIAOZSCKI
YEB LGGVMGGVZ GDSZAFF ZAU
MGGVZ SEOAA SG GKA.
                    —F.H. MGBI

163. BXVK QUM GVDD CVDDVMKOS
VMZ CAZT GVDD VZHDKUOS YT
QHGX QAOU GAQQAM BXUOU
KXU GDYQVKU YT THDKOS.

—DAOZ RSOAM

164. GQX KQYOOI PYOW PJ ZJGQX UDNP
NJ PSQI AYX NOQQC ZLPS PSQG YXV
ZJGQX NOQQC ZLPS GQX UDNP NJ
PSQI AYX PYOW PJ PSQG.

—UYI GALXQKXQI

165. GV GJRUWQ-DK-BIX PQJEW NM GV
GIQQDIYW. JKW TIV GV XDZW FIGW
UJGW WIQBV ZQJG XJQE IKT ZJNKT NH
DK PWT RJYWRUWQ.   —BWKKV PQNFW

166. VDB AGHH FS PS DBZ HIBFPY
CSX JIRQDH GBPIXWSQXJI. YI
AGHH XGJU CSXPQBI, WYDXDWPIX,
XIMQPDPGSB — HGCI GPJIHC.

—VDXU PADGB

Harder, Harder

167. G'HT FRTVM YPRJ EGMA NTP
G'HT UTTP NOSSGTL MY. AYE
NOPJ EYNTP BOP AYPTFMRJ
FMOMT MAOM BROGN?

—TRGKOUTMA MOJRYS

168. DSB VJNBVO DSTEC LUJRD
UBTEC GJXDO TZ DSLD OJR WLE
LAAXBWTLDB DFBEDO-GTNB-OBLX-JVH
KBE KJXB.   —WJVVBBE KWWRVVJRCS

169. LM DAZKC VEUWD JMY
UEJMJJZHMFG MYRMND QWTZKP DAM
NAGJZRVF VRD, LAMK UWT XZKQJ
EMPZK DU LVKQMT.

—AULVTQ KMXMTUH

170. WC HTL HWNPQ WK KEYLR
WBVEMZM, PK MLA KBEFR XLBL E
QBPZL, ZWMH XWZLC XWFDR VW HW
NBPMWC HTL BLMH WK HTLPB DPILM.

—ZLBBPDD ZEBYWL

171. YIP VUZ SULLPNPFWP VPYQPPF
HPA LMN DMFPX TFS HPA LMN LNPP
UH YITY HPA LMN DMFPX KHKTJJX
WMHYH T JMY JPHH.

—VNPFSTF VPITF

172. H RXHYB RXZ FZGSZNR QTKZG
HU UTEZTYZ LXT ROGYU HYRT D
FHIID DR STOG T'NQTNB HY RXZ
ETGYHYJ.   —NXDGQZU FHZGNZ

173. N CBPKRV KT UR B OFNRWK,
UJK CSRP KSRD KTMV LR N ETJMV
PRXRF SBXR WRY — PTK RXRP TP
LD UNFKSVBD — N ESBPIRV LD LNPV.

—GTSPPD XRIBW

174. RE ZKC UVX QRMRBI ARWF U NUB,
ZKC LKB'W FUMX WK AKVVZ UJKCW
AFXWFXV ZKC DFKCQL
DQXXS ARWF FRN UEWXV LRBBXV.

—DWXSFUBRX JVCDF

175. LJCOOS, ZICZ OYZZOJ
UJCOSDHD YW RNXI ZHH VCL
VLHR ZIJ IHOJ. YZ WIHNOU LJCOOS
DJ DNYOZ LYPIZ YF.   —OHLJZZC OSFF

176. U'B FEIQZ STLS U'B GVS
HURCPELF. U WVG'S STUGQ U
IVEFW RSLGW HCUGA XCMCISCW
HZ BCG LR YCFF LR YVBCG.
                        —HCXGLXW BLGGUGA

177. HMMWCZ WTWOJ NSULP PHZW
JKI MHL BWZ, WTWL RUZQ H BUOS
RQK RWHOX AWHLX. FHJNW JKI MHL
ZHSD QWO KIZ KE ZQWF.
                    —HNUBHUS THL NIOWL

178. SKAH ISR LGBRO CO ISCJ
QGMOIXF QKO'I GXZKJB. CH CI
LRXR ISR BKARJ, CI LGMAT YR
TRQAKXRT K OKICGOKA RBRXZROQF.
                        —BKXZG JI. VKBRJ

179. ZUA TJZ MUZDWSUM RC NU ZVCGR,
SJZRH, JSM NGORDZV. DL TVJR HCO
TJSR DZ POMMKDSW, HCO ZVCOKM
NOH J YOYYH.

—EOKDU NOGPVDKK

180. KJAFFCYWO AJLGVUZ, LVJNYWO
WXKVDZ, JWN VJUYWO ASXAXDJUV JLV
XWDP MJPZ XH GJZZYWO UYCV FWUYD
PXF AJW HFAI JOJYW.

—APWUSYJ SVYCVD

181. SZRWVZKZR EFR'W QAZHZA
CVFREZB. X WUXRT XH X YZAZ
YAXWXRS WUPW CFFT WFEPL, X'E
JPVV XW "SZRWVZKZR QAZHZA
SZRWVZKZR."   —PRXWP VFFB

182. H PU TABLVPBVYR PUPCZK FOZB H
VPYW VA RADBS IZAIYZ VA YZPXB OAF
UDTO VOZR WBAF PJADV LZQ PBK OAF
YHVVYZ PJADV LAPI.

—JHYYHZ JDXWZ

183. B IVOESFE ZFBST BHP IFTUFS

QSZOOF XBT HJWFO BO B GPS

BEVMUFSZ. UPEBZ TIF XPVME

TDPSF OP CFUUFS UIBO B D-QMVT.

　　　　　　　　—QFUFS EF WSJFT

184. OSP RO VBSHE, LJE RE'O

GSCSB HO VBSHE HO RE IHO IKSG

MYJ ISBS H QKRFA, IKSG RE IHO

OERFF HFF H LRV XMOESBM.

　　　　　　　　—AHCRA AJQKYCGM

185. OT ZCN'VU HNFPZ UMCNYQ SC

KHUUG JOSQ X GVUSSZ YOVH, AXPU

SQXS ZCNV KUFVUS. SQU LUKS JXZ

SC VNOM OS OK SC SUHH GUCGHU

XLCNS OS.　　　　　—VOG SCVM

186. AE GQRDM'E FNEERI ZORIR

TQJ OAGR TQJI DRV FNLNUAMRD

XRWNJDR TQJI ERRMNLRI ZAHH

FNCR DJIR EQ KAMG EORF.

　　　　　　　　—XIJWR HNMDCT

187. DOZG LC Z PLCC, ZMGEZBBR? Z
JUCR NUG UXIJ GOI "L" UH "BUXLFV."
Z CIMJIG GUBN GU GOI KUEGO
LFCGIZN UH GOI IZJ.

—INKUFN JUCGZFN

188. B XFNL DOP PBFFLE ABUD
QOPXFFO. B AOTF'U FLEMXGT, JGU
ABUDBF OJXGU O QBFGUL B YXGFP
QCTLKY UOKIBFV OJXGU GFPLEALOE.

—EOFPC FLAQOF

189. JWARPAB TELC BPCX'J XEIW
XWUUWCJ UE TELC CPIKX KQUWC
VW VKJ SKCCPWR VWC PJ EAW
WQQWZUPIW QECS EQ CWIWABW.

—KSFCEJW FPWCZW

190. TQ EZIFWE EQVCFBK SZV DK QZ AK
ECMTFB QLTE, AIQ T'PK RZDK QZ QLK
RZFRHIETZF QLCQ EKO VKCHHM TE
SZV NVZRVKCQTZF.

—KVTR RHCNQZF

Harder, Harder

191. F KU FZ XKINM NX NCDGFZS
OLD XMDZVL LKCFO NX YFEEFZS
JKTFDE' LKZTE. KXODM KJJ, NZD
UAEO EOKMO ENUDRLDMD.

— EKVLK SAFOMG

192. U JQRUO ABNTD MTB GTDA AQ
XTA UEE DMT KUO QLA QV U RUO,
UOY U RUO ABNTD MND GTDA AQ
XTA UEE MT KUO NOAQ U JQRUO.

— NDUUK XQEYGTBX

193. OG LKY SANBBL RNDU UK BKKE
FAZL OD N MCKUK, LKY'V WAUUAS
WA UCODEODT NWKYU FAZ SNUCAS
UCND NWKYU WAODT FAZL.

— MAUN ROBFKD

194. LE LG Y GLAR QZ Y VXPP
RYEXNJ EQ SJ QKJNQUUXFLJV YSQXE
JCJNULGJ, JYELRA YRV VNLROLRA,
QN GJCXYP LREJNUQXNGJ.

— JFLUEJEXG

195. ZB OBHTWWTGHYZW OP
PUSTKULI QEU EZP JUYBL
PUSTHEOBC SUXT OBHTXTPHOBC
HU HZWV ZKUYH HEZB PTR.

—ZWLUYP EYRWTI

196. ZJ OSK GLNSWQL XS UZQL
KF NISDZTU, AGZTDZTU, MTA
WSQZTU, OSK AST'X MRXKMWWO
WZQL WSTULG; ZX HKNX NLLIN
WSTULG. —RWLILTX JGLKA

197. VAXOBNXHBO AY PKYXVT
NZKHX YOG NIR IKX PHWF NZKHX
FNUAIQ WFAVRBOI EFAVO VALO AY
XFO KXFOB ENT NBKHIR.

—RNUAR VKRQO

198. UKLH IKL SOYHQVEIKLOX EG
IEQYT'X UEOWQ KLYO IKL UEOQ
"BKMJJLHQYWLX," IKLT HE WEHSLO
RDXI IKMHF EG IKL BKYMOX.

—RLYH FLOO

Harder, Harder

199. Y R H S Z P F   O S Z   E B X R Y S B S X

L B X R Y   O T Y H O E E I   A P   S J Y R B S X

L J F P   Y R O S   T F O V I   K P G   A P Y M P P S

R P O Q P S   O S Z   P O F Y R.

                              —E P J S B Z   K.   K H C R J F H C J Q

200. U I L H L   Y M   W A U I Y W F   U I V U

S A X C V H L M   U A   V   R Y M M   N A W F   V W E

I A U   E A Z W   U A   P A G H   M A G N   U I V U

V N X A M U   C V H V N P K L M   P A G.

                              —T V X L M   T A P S L

201. O I N O G I' F   W V V R V D E I F   W Y N D V

F I J   W C I S' V   L I W G V L Z   W S Z U L I C I,

I J P I O V   T W Z Y I   R S   V L N F I   V C R Y I F

U L I C I   V L I Z   K N   W C N D S E   S W A I E.

                              —W F R W   W C K I S V N

202. H O N   A Q W S O C W W B H O   E L Q P V   A C

T L L P S W F   X L   T L L P   H G L Q O V   E S X F   F S W

W C K G C X H G N.   S T   S X' W   W L B C A L V N

C P W C' W   W C K G C X H G N,   Y L   H F C H V.

                              —A H G G N   Y L P V E H X C G

203. OY ZCNYAIP. SA GQI IFY CE YPYZWNSZ TSONCWQN EYCN XCWYN, GQI XSPP ZQJY CEK HQ CW WLY FCJY WSJY. —PQISFY FCJJQEF

204. CDYS DY'X IFBY HZK QUSSYK, DY'X YUBDYK DFAUSO FS FHHFUK ZK UX IMUSO QYFQ US BDY XBKYYB. U FICFMX DZGY UB'X BDY XBKYYB. —EYXXUPF BFSQM

205. UZ UH VEN VW ZIN HAMNLHZUZUVEH VW ZIN IAKJE KUEX ZV IJYN UKJDUENX ZIJZ YULDUEUZP SVAOX TN J YULZAN. —YVOZJULN

206. QFMMFRN FM O XYORM SA NYIIFRN IHS DYSDKY MS BKSMY ISNYIUYW IUOI IUYL BOR'I MYY ORLIUFRN HWSRN HFIU YOBU SIUYW. —WYRY LOMYRYQ

Harder, Harder

207. QLVMI CJM C UJLNZMV, NPE YS
ALP GCWMI'E CZJMCKA OPMTTMK,
EGMA CJM EGM BYIK LS UJLNZMV Y
MIFLA QJMTEZYIO QYEG.

—QCJJMI NMCEEA

208. R VIQN I KYLWJN ZPIPTN LC
FDZNAC, WIBNX. R VIQN PVNZN
YNIAAD KRS MTYAZ IWX UIPNY
MLFNZ LTP LC NQNYD MTYA. RP'Z
VLP.

—FIMD SYID

209. QV GSS BYI AQFSO GBBIXNQXA
BYI PGSI JFLH RIFI SGQN IXN BL IXN,
QB RLKSNX'B GB GSS OKFJFQOI HI.

—NLFLBYP JGFMIF

210. YR LVKKSGVVC, E ADENKZD
YA GLED FZVFKZ UEKK ERS GVJER
ORCZN DLYNDS GLV YA RVD
EUDYQZKS ZJFKVSZC YR E INVDLZK.

—IZR LZULD

211. FRILUHRILMQULK XRLF UI
LVR DMK NG QUGR; VND HMIK LUHRF
VMZR DR XNIR NYL QNNEUIX GNP
FRC MIT GNYIT NIQK QNZR?

—GPRISV DMQQ

212. CUCBXITGLQ KRJWI NTJLC VCP
GV ZJLHCBDWY. CPMCNI DJB ITC
NKBI ZTCBC ZC DGQTI JUCB ZTJ
QCIV IJ RC ITC BCMCGUCB.

—VTKZL FCLLCHX

213. CGROR UPRV JE PAM VJSWEU,
JEM 'CDJV VGORDMAS VJWM,
"PAM BWVG JC CGR CJIAR, IZC
SPZEU BARVG WE IRM."

—JARQJEMRO FPFR

214. IPY'W YPTLG EHVI KW RKILZLWW
PYG LRLVYPZ PYG FPY QL ZHHTLG
JAHY UKRM CHS QS ALHAZL HE PZZ
PXLW.   —PJXJWRL VHGKY

215. IUZZ AU TYPI P APV CBVHO
OUGWPZZL PIIMPFIBKU PVH B TBZZ
IUZZ LXW YBO UVIBMU JYBZXOXJYL
XC ZBCU.   —PLV MPVH

216. JU'T MJCFSBUJOH UP CF OBLFE JO
GSPOU PG B IVOESFE QFPQMF, CVU
UIFSF'T OPUIJOH TFYVBM BCPVU
MPWFNBLJOH PO B NPWJF TFU.
                           —CJMM QBYUPO

217. HYY KIMWWMW HIM GMIMYR
UHIJHNJPCW PC NOM MNMICHY
WNIVLLYM EMNQMMC KMWJIM NP
KIMWW HCK NOM KMWJIM NP EM
VCKIMWWMK.   —YJC RVNHCL

218. NOSY'B LMENM SB BCJ RWDXC
DB MEYODMF AEWC YOSM YOC
AEYEW ACAEWZ EI HWCXDEKBQZ
CJHCWDCMGCR HQCSBKWC.
                      —NDQQDSA WCDGO

219. D X W A W   K W O   Y X V   I V   G E V P O H
W T C Z G M O M O I   X V Y   D X W L   Y E M D W
C V W K A   . . .   M D ' A   Z M N W   W T C Z G M O M O I
X V Y   L V P   A Z W W C   Y M D X   L V P E   Y M J W .

— C X M Z M C   Z G E N M O

220. N Q ' G   T   P D N W R F G T U U Z   K R U I
C A N D N C D   Q K T Q   R W R F Z   J C B T D   N G
C D U Z   Q J C   I F N D S G   T J T Z   V F C B   T
L N F U - C D - L N F U   T I W R D Q P F R .

— I T W N I   G A T I R

221. J   Q R P ' A   S N T L .   J ' G L   F R A
E R T C R P L K   N P Q   K L I   J K   A E L T L ,   K R
M E O   P R A ?   K L I   J K   F R R Q .   L G L T O Z R Q O
Q R L K   J A ,   N P Q   L G L T O Z R Q O   K E R B X Q .

— T R Z Z J L   M J X X J N C K

222. O ' P   I X C   K C A M H U   P H M I   Q O R C Q W   I H
M Q C C K   Y O I X   P W   L C P D Q C   L D U M .
O   S N M I   J C U N O U C Q W   Q H F C   H I X C A
Y H P C U .   I X C W   R U H Y   I X D I .

— D U J C Q O U D   S H Q O C

223. ZFC WZ DFJIEDZ OWVF
HTOUTJF: E OTCTJN UIEU KBON
AFHKLFZ EB EJU EYUFJ PFBFJEUWKBZ
KY OFWZTJFON EHHFDUEBHF.

                    —EOWHF A. UKVOEZ

224. RQBRJQ DZZLTQ IB RJDM D
ZQCLDJJM BRQY WUDNDWIQN JXGQ
ZDTDYIUD, X TLZI UDSQ UDH
ADFLJBLZ ZQC ABN TBZI BA TM JXAQ.

                    —GXT WDIINDJJ

225. PON PVPTN "HVRR HVRR MBYK
MBYK" VR LNIOBLR PON MIVNUNRP
RDEEBIC LQRRVMTN QU PON MBRVX
BLLNBT QU EQAVNR.

                    —LBDTVYN HBNT

226. TDK LVKPXNTK ETWPL NZHN
NGT CPJ ZPKLVJA OZPPU GHO GHS
CTKP OPMDHI NZHJ NGT CPJ
ZHQVJA OPM TJ OXKPPJ.

                    —EHWP ASIIPJZHHI

227. XU'J XCC-TWMEDXSF LEQ YS
ECG TQEYG UE JXSF YTEVU REK
TYG JRW KYSUJ XU, TVU
EMMYJXESYCCH KW GE YSHKYH.

—CWSY REQSW

228. GCS PIIY H RIPRI CE ASQCF
HJCSZ RIK, JINHSRI OAIP GCS
XCCV HZ DZ, DZ'R HXX RCQIOAHZ
FDYDNSXCSR, DRP'Z DZ?

—NHZ YIIXIG

229. QEJU'T UEB WCNNBLBXMB
GBUQBBX J QEFLB JXW J
MFXDLBTTZJX? J MFXDLBTTZJX
ZJYBT ZFLB ZFXBR.

—BWQJLW JGGBR

230. TC NRVNIUOTKP HRMR
GUEETVRNN, FRUNKN HRMR GUEETRM
KGUV SRV; FIK GISUV CROTBTKP TN
OZJWRJ TV KGR NZIO, VZK TV KGR
CORNG.

—NRVRBU

Harder, Harder

231. Y S E ' W   N S J   D B E Y   B W
B E W P L P K W B E R   A S F   W A P   K S J E Y K
G L P   W A P   K G Z P   D S L   G E   G F D J X
E B R A W Z G L P   G E Y   R L P G W   K P V ?

—L J P   Z U U X G E G A G E

232. E O I   T D M J F D K   X L C Q E M P C   P X
J L Z Q S I   M Z   E P   T L S S   F C U   C P E   E P
T L Z O ,   I G Q I T E   M C   E O I   Q F Z I   P X   E O I
Y I C M E F S Z   F C U   E O I   E P C Y L I .

—S I P C F D U P   U F   H M C Q M

233. Q E   X D N S A R O Q E J ,   R T   Q E
C F S   D C F S W   R W C T ,   C F D T S   H D
Q C   I S T C   Z F D   Y R E E D C   C S X X
F D Z   Q C   Q T   H D E S .

—P R A S T   A .   I R W W Q S

234. G ' D   T L   C J S C P Q M   V G U E   V L D O J
U E F U   G Z   G   V F T   U L   Z F S S   G J U L   F
H F I I O S   L Z   J G K K S O T ,   G ' R   P L D O   L C U
T C P Q G J Y   D M   U E C D H .

—Z I O R R G O   T U F I I

235. EAI PNTT NT U FDQCGITT
UQENBLGUENDR DK CITNQI FADTI
DYSIBE GNIT NR EAI KLELQI, URC
TDOIFAUE ED EAI TDLEA.

—GURBI ODQQDF

236. Y DXF JXLO WVAO ZVH
OYCKN KVGHI. QGN NKYI
YFDWGUOI ZVGH KVGHI VZ
QOCCYFC ZVWWVEOU QT UYFFOH
XFU X JVAYO.

—INYFC

237. CJZDPR DY MCYK. DE D NCFM
ZW JXK, D QGYZ ZNDPU WE HK YMB
ADEM, CPO DE D NCFM ZW ACGRN,
D QGYZ ZNDPU WE HK YMB ADEM.

—RAMPOC QCJUYWP

238. SCUW AZTW DZ WTWYR HYZCM RZE
SWWD. OX RZE QWD XOTW NWYFWVD
ZV RZEY ZEDACR, FZVIOMWY OD C
QZZM OVTWIDSWVD.

—CYVZAM HWVVWDD

Harder, Harder

239. HU YWBFTL TF ZL
ZCWEZMSWVTY SWHWFGNBZP,
RSTYS HZJGF TA JTLK WI SZEK
IWE STH AW YWHG WBA WI ASG
YPWFGA.   —VTPP JGPPU

240. W KZVWZUZ YNCY PZL WP
EMZ EG YNZ SEPY KZCXYWGXV,
MCYXICV, ANEVZPESZ YNWMDP
YNCY SEMZQ TCM KXQ.

                    —PYZUZ SCIYWM

241. Z NLUQ AZU LGHQ GZSQX ZKEQN
SQ, VWE EBQ HZEZYLC XQUHNFTEFLG
NQZX: GL CLLX FG VQX, VWE KFGQ WT
ZCZFGUE Z AZYY.

                    —QYQZGLN NLLUQDQYE

242. QUQZIBEQ ODBPO XDQCZ XDBEF
BMX XDQ RJHW BS XDQCZ TQJEO.
IBM'YY FQX J KMHD RQXXQZ YCEQ
CS IBM PQJZ EB WECHWQZO.

                    —UCHXBZCJ RQHWDJK

243. ZBGZXNS GK SRN QBNTSNKS
UTKSGIN QWJ ZBNTSNJ. ZNBSTGAEF
IPZR LNSSNB SRTA KND, TESRWPQR
KND GKA'S SWW LTJ NGSRNB.

—RTBWEJ UGASNB

244. BWUWEBWEGB UZK CEXK U
AEXETE: VLUW WLKM ZKIKUC EB
BRDDKBWEIK ARW VLUW WLKM
GJTGKUC EB IEWUC.

—UUZJT CKIKTBWKET

245. LXBTWXKN XP RYPPXSWT.
ZJNKAXJO XP RYPPXSWT XL NYE'DT
PKESSYDJ ZJB PKDYJO. SEK XK'P
JYK KAZK XURYDKZJK.

—UXMATWWT RLTXLLTD

246. N TFGW F UFUUJJ JZ YB YJOU
CANGFUW CFAU JQ YNEVWB FZK
YNZZNW YJLOW NZGJDGWK NZ F OWM
FEU. NU'O YB OWZOW JQ TLYJA.

—PFZWU PFEVOJZ

247. S D R   J L E E D O   V U L X F
M D T E D K T L M Z S .   Y Z F E   A   Y L W   L
S D R E K   J Z A U B ,   A   R W F B   O D
X L W O R T V L O F   O D   "K A U U A K L E ' W
A W U L E B ."   — T D E   P F T F X S

248. F E J   C A T K   Q A F J N J O F Q A Y   F E Q A Y
F E M F   V M A   E M H H J A   Q A   M   O S Q O O
D J P N C C B   Q O   O W X X C V M F Q C A   D K   M
X J M F E J N   B M F F N J O O .

                    — P M T F C A   F N W B D C

249. U   P U Q Y   H Y Y V .   U   K Y H U J U V Y P B
O W I Y   W   H Y V U T O .   U   P N I Y   V N   T Y Y   W
A W J ' T   F W E Y   H N N V ,   F D V   U V ' T   M N V
V N   F Y   J U Z Y P B   A W J U Z D E Y K .

                    — F E N N Q Y   F D E Q Y

250. T G A X J C   Q V G S V P T T   A J R   M P
F J V I P H   P K J A O C Z   M Z   O W P   T G A X J C
Q G T X O X G R   G L   O W P   L J X V   T P K —
O W P   N S C Z   G R P T   X R A C N H P H .

                    — I J V C   F J V K

251. JCVZUK CGQ VQUIQGJD
QUVNEKZCKVZA. ZU YGCHZJ VNQD
VNGSP XJSPQGK CV DSE. ZU
CGMQUVZUC VNQD VNGSP
VNQLKQJFQK.　　—LCGJQUQ IZQVGZAN

252. X PJLLAGM MRB MRBAGH MRSM
SDHADB ISD EBM FSXZ. XM'P PXCLFH
S CSMMBG AV FAQBGXDE HAJG
PMSDZSGZP BDAJER.

　　　　　　　　　　—CXIRSBF PMXLB

253. DCTVXJ AXDDLFR LD
JXMOCJN XR CSFYLFR FI AFZCM
XRQ QFSLRXYLFR. RFYWLRO DXND,
"SLRC, SLRC" SFMC ILCMHCJN.
　　　　　　—HWXMJCD WFMYFR HFFJCN

254. O EXT X CLFTJOJRJQ UFL
ZFAJBT VQUFLQ OJ BOJ ZQ. O
YOHQW OJ TF ZRKB, O KFRYWA'J
OZXIOAQ OJ EXT CLFTJOJRJOFA.
　　　　　　—XAAOQ TCLOAHYQ

255. WBT LW INB IHQHWMG WHXMB
CNLMN HK HUGRBWMBKI KHILGKHR
ZHRHIB WZYLKJRBW GK BABYF
MGXYWB LK INB SBKX.

—SHYF UHF CLKK

256. HOLVV BILEN UIA BIAKE
QLIYPYKU LPHOVL WIH OVPL
BOJKV UIA'LV YANU TPXJWC KIGV
PLV, "OIWVU! J'T OITV!"

—XVW OPTTIWE

257. SNT OZCTMP SNTZMU AW SNKS
UZY IKP NKXT QZSN BZXT KPC WTL
AP K OKMMAKJT; PZ EMTXAZYW
WZIATSU QTBATXTC SNAW.

—KBKAP CT QZSSZP

258. QD QYBW QFQYGCJZF
XCGWLFG MB CZTCDB WEF
XGFBFLW YLF; WEF GFBW CZZ
QFGUF MLWY C BFC YI JZYLOFB.

—GYO BWFTCGW

259. KN COLH PTHWR'B VXFH CDXB
O PT CDOAH O'K XCXN LFTK DTKH
XW ATRY XW O PTR'B DXZH X YTTP
BOKH CDOAH O'K PTORY OB.

—AHH BFHZORT

260. "FYXUX WYMHNQ MIX HWX
JXUBHZX?" E FMZEI MILX EWSXQ
ZX. "FYXUXRXU MIX FEIKW KM OX
SGWWXQ," G UXJNGXQ.

—LMLM LYEIXN

261. JYAYBHCGOTWZI WB KYF'B
MOI YP WQBGXWQK ZJOZ ZJH
ZXGTI KWPZHF OXHQ'Z NGXFHQHF
MWZJ DJWTFXHQ.   —BOA OGBZWQ

262. YP COSEZD LJ PJM EA WJL LJ
EWHMEFD XKP JF XKELKDF, NML LJ
BMAL DWBJP PJMF EZD ZFDCY XKEUD
EL EA JW PJMF GUCLD.

—LKJFWLJW XEUODF

Harder, Harder

263. KJHSNIZBOMA AIJJH ZM
YEZM NJCA — AQXJ JDJM ZM
AJHOKOYJ KQQXA. YFOY ZA EFG
YFJKJ OKJ XQKJ CJXQBKOYA.

—EZII AYOMYQM

264. FPXM OM QVV OEXXZ QTEPH
HIM DEDPVQHJEK MGDVEFJEK,
TPH OM KMNMX OEXXZ QTEPH JH
QH HIM XJUIH HJYM.

—QXHIPX IEDDM

265. U GRUIL UG'P HYYV GY RKWC
PCA OUGR PYFCYIC ORCI BYE'JC
IYG PEZZYPCM GY. UG'P HYYV GY
XC PICKLB KXYEG UG.

—HKJFCI CVCHGJK

266. GRIVE VIRRV. QIXQRI MXT'A
CPTA AX VII QYSABNIV XG SEBNSEIV.
AEIJ CPTA AX VII TPWIM ZXMYIV.

—EIRIT UYNNIT

267. J PV DYM JMAZVRV, YD
HSPOS IZQPAV SZWA RHY; YKOA
XMPLAQ DYM RSA DCKORPYK,
KYH DYM RSA WPAH.

—MYJAMR XZCI VEPRS

268. FGD PCL'Q ZOCQ NOU
GDQBGGXN. E REYO VGXONQN,
ZCXLN, NAEJJELT SGGR PWCLTELT
XGGJN, GL QGS GV WERRN, FGD
LCJO EQ. —YCQEO SXEPO

269. O'PC NIW NFCTW QDCTPTNC,
NFCTW ETOF, THJ NFCTW DCNG. O
XTMC QCFWTOH WEIGC VOWG TFC
KETW SCISDC'G CBCG TFC JFTKH WI.

—VTFVTFT TWMOH

270. VER CUQB FK X VMAR LMACE UC
VEXV JFA KXII UB IFPR GUVE RXLE
FVERM KUMCV XBN QMFTR KFM
MRXCFBC XKVRMGXMN.

—CEXBX XIRZXBNRM

271. YM MYA ITY CVAAJ NQBX LQIH. XA NTHAC SJ LSOQYE BXA YQEXB, CNQBIXAC MY BXA VQEXBC, TYL CJATHC QYBM XQC BTJA OAIMOLAO.

—JTB YQDMY

272. PHBHU ZHDIGH XHRKLYYA EPBIYBHS VEFC LPAIPH AIK OHPKEPHYA DLUH LZIKF. L XHRKLY UHYLFEIPXCEQ OKLULPFHHX L YIXX.

—GLUA OIUSIP

273. NKRRPVO HJEJSVNR BAPIWSG KOH PR BAPIWJRZ ZV MKHJ. POZPQKIG HJEJSVNR RSVLSG, KOH IVQQPZQJOZ QVDJ UDKHAKSSG RZPSS.

—DVTJDZ RZJDOTJDU

274. CIY UDWYZREV SRUU ZY DAY IJAVEYV KYENYAC XQRCIXJU CD IRP GQCY QP UDAO QP CIYB'EY UDNLYV CDOYCIYE RA CIY PQGY NQOY.

—SRUU NJKKB

275. P RCS BPRZAIX ZHV QAMG
KXRCAGX ZNXIX PG GVEXZNPSQ ZV
QICK NVFJ VL. KAZ NVH JV ZHV
PSGPJXG ECYX FVUX?

—FMJPC FVBVYVUC

276. LQLWUKIF KH WBKLOCX WEVHLP AX
ZEQHFKZH, EQUKWBIJLH, UVQFKZH,
EHZEQEYVH, WEFPKLP YKFYLQ, EFP HI
OIQUB.   —EQKHUIUCL

277. MX ZAXFSMOHOVD OH WLHM COJF
HFY ZVA MZYFH; MRF GISF MZCJ
MRFSF OH ZKILM MRFG, MRF CFHH
COJFCN MRFN ZSF MI KF BLSKFA.

—WZBJ DILCA

278. PUSJG CAH XSD AXYUWP X
PHHT GDV MAUWP GMXB UW WDC
BHSF. MAD SDGM CXWM MH GODWT
MADUS GQKKDS YXEXMUHWG UW
DQSHOD.   —PXUJ OXSDWM

Harder, Harder

279. H ZHCY JYHQF VNIAVVUX. H ZHCY
IV XCHK HQ IBY LVUYXIX HQ IBY
QNAY. HI HX MQVIBYU TVUZA IV IMCY
XNQJMIBX HQ IBY QNAY.

—JYIIHY KMFY

280. Y VDNYB NYP UYEO Y ZMOYBOH
NLBX GUYB Y NYB, RSG GUYG'J DBMP
ROZYSJO JUO ZUYBCOJ UOHJ NDHO
DKGOB.   —DMLEOH UOHKDHX

281. ERAX UBKAIBHM DWOAU
MBG S UANM PBBC, MBG CXBE
YRAM'ZA YZMWXD. IGY ERAX MBG
UKWPA, WY'U UB KGFR UANWAZ.

—FSZBP SPY

282. MLJR MRE — DBPX L UKIQKN,
CWZZRC OSKGRM, LIQ L DRPMWBP —
BM YRCJRUPSA KFLA LM SKIO
LM AKW QKI'P JLSS BI SKGR.

—FRCCA PXKCISRA

283. LBC LBWVY W EWXC UTIL
KJTPL MCEWJKMH WI LBKL HTP ZTV'L
VCCZ LT JTLBCA ACKZWVY LBC
UKVPKE.   —IBCEZTV XCEECA

284. YCD MWJK PDIXMW YCIY U
SMGJT YIED GO QMHHUWH UX XM
YCIY U LMGJT CDIP CDIFK RPDIYCUWH
IHIUW.   —DPBI RMBRDLE

285. YNI SKS FJH LNTJ DN OJ
DYNWUYD NR QF SKEDB KZ DYJ
RKEFD ACQLJ? UNS TWFD YQGJ OJJZ
Q EJAWOCKLQZ.   —IKCC SWEFD

286. M AML YML WMGZ QST, AMUFZ
QWEZZ JTGZ MKKMHEX SWHJZ WZ'X
AMEEHZB. FRQ MKQZE QWMQ, HQ'X
YWZMQHLN.   —UGZX ATLQMLB

287. MNYQ DHI ZFP DKF AKNWDWYX USF
NHYX UCN USLHMZ XNV TDH FHENX
CLUSNVU DTUVDYYX WFLHM DHX MNNI
DU USFB.   —ELBBX IFBDKFU

Harder, Harder

288. RSL NIDRIPV QN LELJV IXPRJIAKID WID KP RQ SIEL RYQ YQWLD — QDL BALIDKDF IDM RSL QRSLJ MXPRKDF.

— WIXJLLD WXJHSV

289. DEGA DGTT SG, "KBQA, DELF LF REGJG RG'JG ZKLWZ DK VPFE PV AKPJ HTGQCQZG," QWX L'S TLBG, "REQD HTGQCQZG?" — WQDQTLG VKJDSQW

290. NJWFWCWI U JWDI MWSMRW AUVXEVVUFL KUIBJ XSFBISR, U DRNDPV IWGWGKWI BJDB U NDV BJW QUQBJ XJURA. — XRDIWFXW ADIISN

291. TYY IATYYP JIATO YEDAIK TIA TIOQMCYTOA, TVZ DAIFTY KAZCMOQEV QK OUA KCIAKO IETZ OE TMOCTY KAZCMOQEV. — XTIPT XTVVAK

292. FNSIMCT TWPZ BCRZIG BCFRMFL; DJMZFLTE TWPZ SZJDZKIZIG MI; VNI XCFIWF TWPZ KWJJNSIZIG CFL ZBVCOZIG MI. — DJCFKMO VCKWF

293. S O F F , L T Z G O J G D A O W T , T J K Y N

O A , A G R S C O L A N , U T T J D Y V L G X O J X ,

G J C C Y J ' A F G N F A V Q O C A P O J X F

R O S T , " G L T N Y V C Y J T N T A ? "

—F Q L N Z G X G B O J T

294. K R F O O E I M D K C O U O G

Q F B B N K J B , O X B E N B E I M S K B E

N J E M J B M . F O O K E I M C D K C O U O G

Q F B B N K J B B M M S E K R K O O K D N J

N E B E C F N J .   —H X U U I F

295. P N F N O R J G S Z D Y H G E I N G

Q D D O Z O N G Z Y S T N P J T D D A P , I R S

Z O D Y ' S I N A Z N U N S T N V Z O P P T D R A O

I N Q Z U N Y T D H N K D B V .   —I Z A A J D P I E

296. Q N R K V Z H K F ? N Z T N P O Z T D J

V K D I K D V Z . Z T D J O D D M J H S H S Z

H G F Z S M N A F D W . N ' A K D U H E E D P A

Z T D E Z H D Q D K J R H A J .

—V P P D T D U T D

Harder, Harder

297. N'F R SMQGGD ESQT SQMOET.

VNUQ BKQT N KRHQ LEEI OQW, GKQ

TQWG IRD N'F LENTL GE GQVV

QHQMDETQ N UTEB.

> —FQVNOOR XERT KRMG

298. FBPPRUZ CUD RC YRTU SURLO

BNBTU ZMPRLO WIMP INL BMEIQCW.

RE RC PIIE ABLBY NIPT NREKIME

BLUCEKUERA.　　　　—BY OIYZCEURL

299. GVZ MGK'A AJV RBMYHBL

VNVYVKA DW AJV PKMQVBGV.

MA'G SPGA AJHA CJVK MA'G

PKWPNWMNNVF, MA CMNN HWWVXA

LDP.　　　　—SHXO KMXJDNGDK

300. X VR KBXWK IB RA SBBR IB

RVYIJSZVIP ZPLBSP X TVCP V DXKTI

DJWUT, XL ABJ GBJDQ DXNP IB

UBRP VWQ GVIUT.

> —YVDCVQBS QVDX

301. OZG UPZ IZPT BCUJ-CPNZGXZH.
XKZT YZJNZIZ NG XKZ KZPZUVXZP. UG
CPBURO NR SKUX XKZT UPZ KZPZ
UVXZP. —UJUG UJXOUG

302. NS GKC YIRW HDBIW ABP,
SNRF I UIDWRBD YLK DBITTG WCDRA
GKC KR. UNTTA IDB ZCAW UDKUA,
IRF UDKUA IDB I FDIH.
—ZIVONB VKTTNRA

303. M NJSCYD'R ZQJZJGU GUW,
YQSVG, JQ MDGPDMRA OJQ
ULUQAHJYA, HSR RBUA'LU PCNPAG
NJQTUY OJQ IU.
—BSDRUQ G. RBJIZGJD

304. LJM LG WEM NAKNJWNVMP
LG ZTKTJV NZLJM TP WENW QLF
ALJ'W ENKM WL RNOM FC TJ WEM
NSUP LG N ZLKMA LJM.
—UNSTLJ PUTWE

Harder, Harder

305. A SHT'N KI EANP WYFIKYVR LDWN
KISHDWI AN'W UZIHN WIO, KISHDWI
YZUHWFW VYT'N BHWN BYTU ITYDUP.
—SYDZNITIR SYO

306. NP LQNLDF ALZP BY L UXBMY
YX UKLJYBJP FLOP FPG. NP RLHP
EU YCP JCLMIPQBPK L HPKD QXMR
YBAP LRX.   —ZLYCBP QPP RBOOXKI

307. BRMXU WMN IOFD IAMN
TUSFDRF VDWH BOSU. VDNS'MN VDN
KRMUV VA CHAJ RK SAO'MN BARHB VA
BNV XWRP.   —TWOX MAPMRBONL

308. T GSKH CAB HYPW KX HKFBS; CABP
HKS'C NKFB HABS CAKD HTVC, YSU
HABS CAKD HKS'C CABP YQB
RYWWTKSYCBVP XKSU.   —CBQBSNB

309. U HUJ DAX GKTXRGR AOHRGZW
DAOZG AG OR OJEXKOPUEGC
UTTNGPOUEGR JXE EAG UNE XW
LGEEOJL CNSJB.   —RUHSGZ QXAJRXJ

For Sexperts Only

310. XG MYYELHFF XF XBF YNL
VHNZVE, BJHL TYOQEL'B NH MHB Z
QXBBQH FYCHBJXLM GYV KHXLM
LZOMJBI?　　　　　—QZOVHL KZTZQQ

311. C KJFOEG GSPCPGQ US C
DGLFCE GLOGBUGSKG UD WCOON
MJB AWCA RJRGSA. AWGS YGBN
DJJS ABJFVEG VGPUSD.
　　　　　　　　—AWG QCECU ECRC

312. GFHH, MLSBF L'DF SFDFC
GNUBIFK NSRYVKR ANXF HVDF
YFZVCF, IVG KV RVW XSVG LZ
RVW'CF KVLSP LU CLPIU?
　　　　　　　　—XFDLS BVMUSFC

313. OWGQMFG EPM LPNWHD
LPOL LPY EOG LM O ZOW'D PYOCL
ND LPCMJKP PND DLMZOBP
VSJWHYF KYMKCOAPG.
　　　　　　　　—CMQYCL QGCWY

314. HFCU XGBSNU, Z SCMBGXVKMKX
SFCXMO GX ZOUMOF AYM GX
WFLLGOW BMCF XFJ LYZO UMK
ZCF.   —HGVLMC NMAOFX

315. W FHUHC HDLHSNHY NI MHH
NEH YTK AEHF ZWCRM AIQRY ZHN
MQFJQCFHY WF NEH LRTSHM NEHK YI
NIYTK.   —AWRR CIZHCM

316. DI DW SDIB RFX JCWWDRTW, CW DI
DW SDIB EDXA CTM SCIAX, IBCI IBAZ
ERXV PRRM WAXUCTIW LFI LCM
VCWIAXW.   —CAWRJ

317. YQD: WOQ RNQEYTLQ CY
SZSQIWELA, WOQ RZYCWCZI
LCVCGTNZTY, EIV WOQ QDRQIYQ
VESIEJNQ.   —NZLV GOQYWQLKCQNV

318. SOZ HJADA LCA ADZAD JK
QCFDMUCJZ OKUDF KJYF QFCZTA; O
RJSOZ HJADA LDFA OKUDF KJYF
TCAADA.   —L.H. SDZMTDZ

319. YT Y'KG UHYFF DAH LB RNJHU AJ PZMYJD HVG UGQAJP UQGJG, Y TYDZMG HVGB'KG UGJH LG HVG IMAJD UQMYRH.   —LGF DYOUAJ

320. B OFIQ YC FIQGBOF BK URGHRBY CA IN XBAQXCKJ WRQHY ACG KFLQP VCIQK BK VQY IFOLBKYCHTQH.
                    —PNXFK YTCIFH

321. DVMQM XB J BNMLXJH NHJLM FGT LJO DGTLV J PGUJO DVJD PXHH WQXZM VMQ LQJAF. VMQ VMJQD.
                    —UMHJOXM EQXRRXDV

322. ER UKU WBDU EX, "KMRWTJMN LBOWT UBJMN JG LBOWT LKJWJMN QBO." J LKJWXU AMWJD J LKG QJQWXXM.   —SGK SGK NKCBO

323. KIR JIQGE C RITCH GIIO CM CH WYWJM VWHPA RPMKIQM NIPHN IBB PHMI TCE NCGWA IB GCQNKMWY?
                    —AMWVKWH OPHN

324. SHIQXSB PDS VH LEZGZXLDL PD
YSWPHZD. X'P ZDYVW NHZ IQDP. X
JSHU QHU IH UQYRJ MDCHU IQD MDCI.

—GYILW RCXSD

325. PEA AYKK J XEIO JFB KWGYUOWFY
HEWQY AWKK YUYQO CETU RYRGYU,
IEU WO WX NTXO JX DEEB JX
IWFDYUX. —NTHYFJK

326. EPQ CE VLWP PQXCSCKN LK SBP
EXWPPK ZKT HPSGPPK SBP JZNPE
SBZK CS CE HPSGPPK SBP EBPPSE.

—ZKTM GZWBLF

327. QTHOTYI DZGH'S QTYUFGSGFN
IDWG. D WZLGHO TW YLHG XDI
XGDZLHK THG XJGH JG KTS JLS EN D
EAI. —ETE ZAELH

328. EJX IPRE VPIUMEZN TZMX UMB
LPIUM XSXV RUZG EP IX ZM OXG LUR,
"UVX BPY RYVX BPY'VX MPE U NPD?"

—TUVVB OVPLM

329. QIT QW GXT IKHTJG GXKIOJ
NYQRG DNJGRCYNGKQI KJ GXNG
ZQR UQI'G XNMT GQ UCTJJ RE WQC
KG. —GCRDNI HNEQGT

330. PUQ, EUJ BYORU QUI, MFOM'Q
FAS SU OYU. KM'Q SFP MFU LUJKQ
KQ QFOLUC NKZU O BAELOQQ JUUCNU.
—LUMUY EBJKBFAN

331. PC YAUB UMJ JA JPMHH YZMY
YZXC YMDIZY XOXSCABX KSEOXS'J
XK MBK JXR XK EB YZX JMPX VMS.
—PMSC JDX YXSSC

332. AYF APSOZVWXR AYWXR CZSOA
QI DWTF WM AYCA MYF'M C DYSPF
WX AYF LWANYFX CXK C NSSL WX
ZFK. —RFSTTPFI RSPFP

333. MOWZ EU ICJN CR RLGWJ, ROW
XNWYRWR EW Y NCQQNW, GBQ MOWZ
ROW CR VJBZA, ROW VWNCIOQR EW.
—XJLXWJQCBR

For Sexperts Only

334. AP ATI SDAML, NIW MN OFNA DL
TPYN E'PIFBYI; AP ATI DLRSP-NDWPL,
NIW MN D UDYUIKFI.

— RIPYRI OIDL LDATDL

335. G'N B YHE NBAZGJH DKL CKUZ
RHJOHLY. GU'Y BWW SHLX
HEZBTYUGJR. G JHHO B WKU KD
YWHHF. — LTFHLU HSHLHUU

336. QY'X YVD FJJW FQSKX YVHY TDDG
YVD WQHSQDX; YVD MHW FQSKX
EDUDS VHUD YVD YQID.

— YHKKRKHV MHETVDHW

337. NF UPWKCXE LW TRJNCX.
RGRJF XLTUA L EJRWW PS ILVR
SZICXE CXE IRA ULN LXGCER NR.

— KRAAR NLEIRJ

338. AMLB EP NGPR C PIPRBU YMS
DBRREWD PMUBJMFI RM VCAA IMG
FCSAEWD CYRBS PBK.

— NGAECW JCSWBP

339. S'E UKH QWQSULH PQFB-UQZNC
WSVFL. QH FNQLH UKH UNQVFD QL
KBHNU QL S'C FSZN HK XN.

                              —XNUUD PSFF

340. YKKE UVJ SVVN EKYD HRC KWEVW
CZVU CK TVOPV CZV WKKU ERWBJY
TKPVUOSBJY.

                              —VWBSO WBCCVW

Solutions

Threesome #1:

1. My love life is terrible. The last time I was inside a woman was when I visited the Statue of Liberty. —Woody Allen

2. It's quality not quantity that counts. But if the quantity drops below once every eight months, I would definitely look into it.

3. Sex between a man and a woman can be absolutely wonderful, assuming you get between the right man and the right woman.

Threesome #2:

1. I could just live without it all. Love with its blood pump, sex with its messy hungers, men with their wet tongues in my ear. —Erica Jong

2. Men have always detested women's gossip because they suspect the truth: their measurements are being taken and compared.

3. After the first ten minutes of a porno, I want to go home and screw. After the first twenty minutes, I never want to screw again as long as I live.

Threesome #3:

1. I said to my doctor the other day, "My penis is burning." He said, "That's because someone is talking about it." —Garry Shandling

2. Oysters are supposed to enhance your sexual performance, but they don't do anything for me. Maybe I put them on too soon.

3. I don't consider myself kinky, but occasionally I like to put on a robe and stand in front of a tennis ball machine.

Threesome #4:

1. There's nothing wrong with making love with the lights on. Just be sure that the car door is closed. —George Burns

2. Happiness? A good martini, a good cigar, a good meal, and a good woman—or a bad woman, depending on how much happiness you can handle.

3. It's difficult getting used to these changing times. I can remember when the air was clean and the sex was dirty.

Threesome #5:

1. My classmates would copulate with anything that moved, but I never saw any reason to limit myself. —Emo Philips

2. You don't appreciate a lot about school, like being spanked every day by a middle-aged woman—stuff you pay good money for later in life.

3. Last night I discovered my wife in bed with another man and I was crushed. So I said, "Get off me, you two!"

Threesome #6:

1. My wife met me at the door the other night in a sexy negligee. Unfortunately, she was just getting home. —Rodney Dangerfield

2. I'm at an age where food has taken the place of sex in my life. In fact, I've just had a mirror put over my kitchen table.

3. My wife's jealousy is getting ridiculous. The other day she looked at my calendar and wanted to know who May was.

Threesome #7:

1. A woman is sometimes a satisfactory substitute for masturbation, but it takes a lot of imagination to make it work. —Karl Kraus

2. There is no unhappier creature on earth than a fetishist who yearns for a woman's shoe and has to embrace the whole woman.

3. Sex education is legitimate in that girls cannot be taught soon enough how children don't come into the world.

Threesome #8:

1. The other night I was making love to my wife and she kept crying, "Deeper, deeper!" So I started quoting Nietzsche to her. —Dennis Miller

2. My wife and I had an airbag installed on the headboard of our bed, and I'm firmly convinced it saved my life.

3. Nothing is more fascinating to me than my own orgasm, and nothing is less fascinating to me than yours.

Threesome #9:

1. Be careful that you don't gallop ahead, leaving her behind. And be sure that she doesn't reach the finish before you do. —Ovid

2. Do not let too strong a light come into your bedroom. A great many things are enhanced by being seen only in a half-light.

3. I hate a woman who offers herself because she ought to do so, and, cold and dry, thinks of her sewing when she's making love.

Threesome #10:

1. From the moment I was six I felt sexy, and believe me it was hell, sheer hell, waiting to do something about it. —Bette Davis

2. A slightly exposed shoulder emerging from a long satin nightgown often packs more sex than two naked bodies in bed.

3. The act of sex, gratifying as it is, is God's joke on humanity. It is just man's desperate attempt at superintendency.

Threesome #11:

1. There is hardly anybody whose sex life, if broadcast, would not fill the world at large with surprise and horror. —W. Somerset Maugham

2. A man marries to have a home, but also because he doesn't want to be bothered with sex and all that sort of thing.

3. Don't you find it interesting how the Tasmanians, who never committed adultery, are now extinct?

Threesome #12:

1. Love thy neighbor. And if he happens to be tall, debonair, and devastating, it will be that much easier. —Mae West

2. How tall are you? Six feet, seven inches, huh? Well let's forget about the six feet and talk about those seven inches.

3. Sex is like playing a game of bridge. If you don't have a good partner, you better have a good hand.

Threesome #13:
1. My husband had a heart attack and I'm afraid I'm to blame. While we were making love, I took the bag off my head. —Joan Rivers
2. All my mother told me was, "The man goes on top and the woman underneath." For three years my husband and I slept on bunk beds.
3. A man can sleep around, no questions asked. Yet when a woman makes nineteen or twenty mistakes, she's a tramp.

Threesome #14:
1. I understand companionship. I understand bought sex in the afternoon. I cannot understand the love affair. —Gore Vidal
2. Sex is. Sex builds no roads, writes no novels, and sex certainly gives no meaning to anything in life but itself.
3. I don't know if my first sexual experience was heterosexual or homosexual. I was too polite to ask.

Threesome #15:
1. My husband said, "Show me your boobs," and I had to pull up my skirt, so it was time to get them done. —Dolly Parton
2. I do have large tits. Always had them. I've pushed them up, whacked them around. Why not make fun of them? I've made a fortune with them.
3. I was the first woman to burn my bra. It took the fire department four days to put it out.

Threesome #16:
1. My father told me all about the birds and the bees. The liar—I went steady with a woodpecker until I was twenty-one. —Bob Hope
2. They are doing things on the screen these days that the French don't even put on postcards.
3. Happiness is watching the television at your girlfriend's house during a power failure.

Threesome #17:
1. I once went on a date and asked the woman if she'd brought any protection. She pulled a switchblade on me. —Scott Roeben
2. Sex is similar to art. Most of it is pretty bad, and the really good stuff is out of your price range.
3. What is by far the most popular pastime in this country? Autoeroticism, hands down.

• •

1. Any man who can drive safely while kissing a pretty girl is simply not giving the kiss the attention it deserves. —Albert Einstein

2. When two people make love, there are at least four present—the two actually there and the two they're thinking about. —Sigmund Freud

3. Nothing prevents me from concentrating. You could put an orgy in my office and I wouldn't look up. Well, maybe once. —Isaac Asimov

4. There's very little advice in men's magazines because men think, "I know what I'm doing. Just show me somebody naked." —Jerry Seinfeld

5. All these ads for the Wonderbra. Is that really a problem in this country? Men not paying enough attention to women's breasts? —Hugh Grant

6. I've made so many movies playing a hooker that they don't pay me in the regular way anymore. They leave it on the dresser. —Shirley MacLaine

7. At eight, my favorite book was "Everything You Always Wanted to Know About Sex But Were Afraid to Ask." I wasn't afraid to ask. —Drew Barrymore

8. Onstage nudity is disgusting and shameful. But if I were twenty with a great body, it'd be artistic, tasteful, and patriotic. —Shelley Winters

9. Penguins mate for life. They all look alike. It's not like they're gonna meet a better-looking penguin someday. —Ellen Degeneres

10. My wife insists on turning off the lights when we make love. That doesn't faze me. It's the hiding that seems so cruel. —Jonathan Katz

11. Nudist beaches? Most people look better with their clothes on, and the few that don't look better than you, so why bother? —Peter Buck

12. Doctors say many men have allergic reactions to latex condoms. They cause severe swelling. So what's the trouble? —Dustin Hoffman

13. Clinton lied. A man might forget where he parks or where he lives, but he never forgets oral sex, no matter how bad it is. —Barbara Bush

14. I love the lines men think will get us into bed. "Please? I'll only stick it in for a minute." What am I, a microwave? —Beverly Mickins

15. My ears turn me on like nothing else. They're my most erogenous zone. Just having them kneaded is like a full-body massage. —Rebecca Romijn

16. Research shows that the more sex a man has, the more he wants. It also shows the less sex a man has, the more he wants. —Conan O'Brien

17. You don't need a language in common for sexual rapport. And it helps if the language you don't understand is Italian. —Madonna

18. During my very first kiss, the girl injected a pound of saliva into my mouth. When I walked away I had to spit it all out. —Leonardo DiCaprio

19. There's nothing wrong with going to bed with someone of your own sex. Be very free with sex—just draw the line at goats. —Elton John

20. Electric flesh-arrows traverse the body. A rainbow strikes the eyelids. A foam of music falls over the ears. The gong of the orgasm. —Anaïs Nin

21. When you really don't like a guy, he'll be all over you, and as soon as you act like you like him, he's no longer interested. —Beyoncé Knowles

22. Size does matter. While there are a lot of ways to make people feel good, I personally think size does enhance things. —Pamela Anderson

23. It wasn't sex appeal but the obvious liking she took to devouring the hamburger that made my pulse hammer with excitement. —Ray Kroc

24. Today's youth are moving away from feeling guilty about sleeping with someone to feeling guilty if they are not. —Margaret Mead

25. Sex should be a wholly satisfying experience from which participants emerge unanxious, rewarded, and ready for more. —Alex Comfort

26. You gotta learn that if you don't get it by midnight, chances are you ain't gonna get it. And if you do, it ain't worth it. —Casey Stengel

Solutions

27. It doesn't matter what you do in the bedroom as long as you don't do it in the streets and frighten the horses. —Mrs. Patrick Campbell

28. Jennifer and I act well. But when the day's over, she goes home to her boyfriend and I go home to a magazine. —David Schwimmer

29. Any idiot can get laid when they're famous. That's easy. It's getting laid when you're nobody that takes some talent. —Kevin Bacon

30. My breasts are beautiful, and I gotta say: they've gotten a lot of attention for what's relatively short screen time. —Cindy Crawford

31. I wouldn't be good at an orgy. I'd probably find myself yelling, "Would somebody please touch me for once! This is my house!" —John Bush

32. Reading computer manuals without the software is frustrating, like reading sex manuals without the hardware. —Arthur C. Clarke

33. A woman who's good in bed shares the creativity of Disney, the imagination of de Sade, and the stamina of Secretariat. —Billy Crystal

34. I had the upbringing a nun would be jealous of. Until I was fifteen I was more familiar with Africa than my own body. —Joe Orton

35. If we make contact with life on other planets, I wonder if they'll be as obsessed with their own genitals as we are. —Albert Brooks

36. Our culture's definition of being lovable is essentially a mixture between being popular and having sex appeal. —Erich Fromm

37. You know, we grope differently on set than we do in real life. On-set groping is far more disgusting than real-life groping. —Kelly Ripa

38. Pornography arouses sexual desires. If pornography is a crime, when will they arrest makers of perfume? —Richard Fleischer

39. The ability to make love frivolously is the chief characteristic which distinguishes human beings from beasts. —Heywood Broun

40. If I'm not into a woman, I'm straightforward. Right after sex I usually say, "I can't do this anymore. Thanks for coming over." —Vince Vaughn

41. A skirt is no obstacle to extemporaneous sex, but it is physically impossible to make love to a woman wearing trousers. —Helen Lawrenson

42. Your marriage is in trouble if your wife says, "You're only interested in one thing," and you can't remember what it is. —Milton Berle

43. I chased a girl two years only to discover that her tastes were exactly like mine: We were both crazy about girls. —Groucho Marx

44. An English jury won't convict for sodomy. Half of them don't believe it can be done, and the other half are doing it. —Winston Churchill

45. Love is the delightful interval between meeting a beautiful girl and discovering that she looks like a haddock. —John Barrymore

46. We of the FBI have no power to act in cases of oral-genital intimacy, unless it in some way obstructs interstate commerce. —J. Edgar Hoover

47. The true test of pornography: Get twelve men to read the book and ask if they got an erection. If most say yes, it's pornographic. —W.H. Auden

48. It has to be admitted that we English have sex on the brain, which is a very unsatisfactory place to have it. —Malcolm Muggeridge

49. My psychologist told me that a lot of men suffer from premature ejaculation, but that's not true. Women suffer. —Robert Schimmel

50. If you're ever in doubt as to whether you should kiss a cute girl, always give her the benefit of the doubt. —Thomas Carlyle

51. The only trouble with sexually liberating women is that there aren't enough sexually liberated men to go around. —Gloria Steinem

52. I wanted to be either a piano player in a whorehouse or a politician. And to tell the truth, there isn't much difference. —Harry S. Truman

53. Sex is a conversation carried out by other means. If you get on well out of bed, half the problems of bed are solved. —Peter Ustinov

54. For women, the best aphrodisiacs are words. The G-spot is in the ears. He who looks for it below there is wasting his time. —Isabel Allende

55. Housework is like bad sex. Every time I do it I swear I will never do it again. Until the next time company comes. —Marilyn Sokol

56. My favorite thing in the world is a box of fine European chocolates, which is definitely much better than sex. —Alicia Silverstone

57. I think pop music has revolutionized oral intercourse more than anything else that has ever happened, and vice versa. —Frank Zappa

58. Women are the strongest magnets in the universe; men are simply cheap metal. And we can all agree where north is. —Larry Miller

59. I grew up in the sixties. Your hair had to be straight and you had to be skinny and have no boobs. It was like not my era. —Bernadette Peters

60. Women complain about sex more often than men. Their gripes fall into two major categories: not enough, and too much. —Ann Landers

61. One misjudgment is that to be a good lover, the guy must have a humongous penis and an erection you can strike matches on. —Sue Johanson

62. I was in Europe and began to fall in love with Americans in uniform. And I continue to have that love affair. —Madeleine Albright

63. In adolescence, pornography is a substitute for sex, whereas in adulthood sex is a substitute for pornography. —Edmund White

64. The advantage of being celibate is that when you see a pretty girl, you need not grieve over having an ugly one at home. —Paul Leautaud

65. Amazingly, the human race has taken enough time from thinking about food or sex to create all the arts and sciences. —Mason Cooley

66. When men turn thirteen and suddenly reach puberty, they think they like women. Actually, you're just horny. —Jules Feiffer

67. It used to be you'd be embarrassed to get condoms, but buying cigarettes was okay. Now it's the other way around. —Jackie Mason

68. We made a plan at school to meet in her garage and kiss. It was like a little business deal. I kissed her then I ran home. —Brad Pitt

69. Sex concentrates on what's on the outside of the individual. It's funny because I think it's better on the inside. —Alex Walsh

70. Making eye contact during rough sex is roughly equivalent to trying to read Dostoyevsky on a roller coaster. —Jenna Jameson

71. The first kiss is magic, the second intimate, the third routine. After that you just take the girl's clothes off. —Raymond Chandler

72. Religion is, after sex, the second oldest resource which human beings have available to them for blowing their minds. —Susan Sontag

73. My boobs were bigger than all my friends' and I was afraid to show them. Now I just feel they're like an accessory. —Jessica Simpson

74. You can't remember sex. You can remember the fact of it, recall where it was and the details, but the sex cannot be remembered. —E.L. Doctorow

75. Men wake up aroused and women think, "How can he want me when I look this way?" There's no blood anywhere near our optic nerve. —Andy Rooney

76. Sometimes you really dig a girl the moment you kiss her but then you get distracted by things like her older sister. —John Sebastian

77. I'm in favor of calling sex something else, and it should include everything from kissing to sitting close together. —Shere Hite

78. I can't even find someone for a platonic relationship, much less the kind where someone wants to see me naked. —Gilbert Gottfried

79. A website had my head on others people's naked bodies. But the real shock was that my body is much nicer. —Nicollette Sheridan

80. There's something very sexy about being submissive. Your guard is down, so you have to totally surrender yourself. —Eva Longoria

81. An excellent sermon should be like a skirt: short enough to arouse interest but long enough to cover the essentials. —Ronald Knox

82. Why does a man assume a girl who flirts wants him to kiss her? Nine times out of ten, she only wants him to want to kiss her. —Helen Rowland

83. People think I sleep with everyone, but I'm not like that. I like kissing, but that's all. I'm not having sex for a year. —Paris Hilton

84. When men have money and power they get turned on sexually. They get horny as hell. I can't imagine why, though. —Penelope Spheeris

85. An archaeologist is the best husband any woman can have; the older she gets, the more interested he is in her. —Agatha Christie

86. People who say gratuitous sex is no substitute for gratuitous violence obviously haven't had enough gratuitous sex. —Geoff Spear

87. "G" means the hero gets the girl. "R" means the villain gets the girl. But "X" means everybody gets the girl. —Kirk Douglas

88. When people say, "You're breaking my heart," they usually just mean that you're breaking their genitals. —Jeffrey Bernard

89. I kissed my first girl and smoked my first cigarette on the same day. I haven't had time for tobacco since. —Arturo Toscanini

90. Men have only two feelings: hungry and horny. I tell my wife, "If I don't have an erection, make me a sandwich." —Bobby Slayton

91. I told her the thing I loved most about her was her mind. That's what I told her to get into bed with me naked. —Steven Wright

92. I've just gone through so much in my life that pulling my top up just doesn't seem like that big of a deal. —Nicole Richie

93. During my army examination, they asked me if I was homosexual. I said I wasn't but I was willing to learn. —Bill Murray

94. The problem is, God equipped us with a penis and a brain, but not enough blood to use both at the same time. —Robin Williams

95. Science is very similar to sex. Sometimes something useful comes of it, but that's not the reason we're doing it. —Richard Feynman

96. In breeding cattle, you need just one bull for every twenty-five cows. Unless the cows are known sluts. —Johnny Carson

97. I'm like a menu at a really expensive restaurant. You can look at me all you please, but you can't afford me. —Anna Kournikova

98. If you consider wearing a push-up bra to an audition manipulation, then yes, I could be called a manipulator. —Alyssa Milano

99. I think it's about time we voted for senators with breasts. After all, we've been electing boobs long enough. —Claire Sargent

100. How lucky we are that we can reach our genitals instead of that spot on our back that itches. —Flash Rosenberg

101. Whenever women catfight, all the boys are secretly hoping it will eventually turn into sex. —Yasmine Bleeth

102. I have no illusions of being a sex symbol. I don't have packs of women chasing me down the street like Brad Pitt or someone. —Tobey Maguire

103. If I were gay, I'd sleep with Leonardo DiCaprio. But only for the long hair he had in "The Man in the Iron Mask." —Ben Affleck

104. Today you see girls doing on the screen what they used to do off the screen to get on the screen. —Gene Autry

105. My husband said to me, "I can't remember when we last had sex," and I said, "Well I can and that's why we ain't doing it." —Roseanne Barr

106. Guys aren't attracted to me because of my mind. They're attracted to me because of what I don't mind. —Gypsy Rose Lee

107. The best sex education for kids is when daddy pats mommy on the fanny when he comes home from work. —William H. Masters

108. Sex is greatest when it's like basketball: one-on-one with as little dribbling as possible. —Leslie Nielsen

109. The best part about being in a relationship is having somebody right there to do it with when you're horny. —Jenny McCarthy

110. Men would sleep with a bicycle providing it had the right color lip gloss on. They have no shame. —Tori Amos

111. Scientists now believe that the primary biological function of breasts is to make males stupid. —Dave Barry

112. I have two ambitions in life: one is to drink every pub dry, the other is to sleep with every woman on earth. —Oliver Reed

113. There is probably no sensitive heterosexual alive who isn't preoccupied with his latent homosexuality. —Norman Mailer

114. I wish I'd invented blue jeans. They have expression, modesty, sex appeal, simplicity—all I want in my clothes. —Yves Saint Laurent

115. If I'd had as many love affairs as I've been credited for, I'd be in a jar at Harvard Medical School. —Frank Sinatra

116. Older women are the best at making love: they always think they may be doing it for the last time. —Ian Fleming

117. The best way to succeed with the opposite sex is by telling her you're impotent. She can't wait to disprove it. —Cary Grant

118. Some condoms are made of sheep intestines, yet I was so scared the first time I wore the whole sheep. —Danny Williams

119. There may be many things better than sex, and some things may be worse. But there's nothing exactly like it. —W.C. Fields

120. Tomorrow is National Meat-Out Day. It's being sponsored by vegetarians, not exhibitionists. —David Letterman

121. Cable TV sex channels don't expand our horizons, don't make us better people, and don't come in clearly enough. —Bill Maher

122. I don't always wear underwear, especially in the heat. If I'm wearing a flower dress, why do I need underwear? —Naomi Campbell

123. I've never had to pretend to be having sex with anyone. I guess I'm just queen of the foreplay dissolve. —Julia Roberts

124. Love is two minutes and fifty-two seconds of squishing noises that shows your mind isn't clicking right. —Johnny Rotten

125. A kiss is a lovely trick designed by nature to stop speech when words become superfluous. —Ingrid Bergman

126. Scratch most feminists and underneath is a woman longing to be a sex object. That's just not all she wants to be. —Betty Rollin

127. Many women said to me, one way or another, that they thought it was sex, not youth, that's wasted on the young. —Janet Harris

128. You know why God is probably a man? Because if God were a woman, she would have made sperm taste like chocolate. —Carrie Snow

129. Why should we take advice on sex from the pope? If he knows anything about it, he shouldn't! —George Bernard Shaw

130. I can't do the same thing every night, the same gestures. That'd be like putting on dirty panties every day. —Brigitte Bardot

131. There's nothing better than good sex. But bad sex? A peanut butter and jelly sandwich is better than bad sex. —Billy Joel

132. When you're a girl with big breasts and a great hot body with six women who aren't, you could say that's a handicap. —Jeff Probst

133. As I grow older and older and totter toward the tomb, I find that I care less and less who goes to bed with whom. —Dorothy L. Sayers

134. If God had intended for everybody to have group sex, I guess he'd have given us all more organs. —Malcolm Bradbury

135. The trouble with censors is that they worry if a girl has cleavage. They ought to worry if she hasn't any. —Marilyn Monroe

136. Great sex is wonderful while it's happening, but who remembers great sex they had in nineteen eighty-three? —Bob Seger

137. I know I say I don't sleep with married men, but what I mean is that I don't sleep with happily married men. —Britt Eklund

138. Masturbation is nothing to be ashamed of, but it's nothing to be particularly proud of either. —Matt Groening

139. Sex appeal is fifty percent what you've got and fifty percent what people think you've got. —Sophia Loren

140. There was a girl knocking on my hotel room door all night last night. I finally had to let her out of my room. —Henny Youngman

141. Being a sex symbol has to do with an attitude, not looks. Most men think it's looks; women know otherwise. —Kathleen Turner

142. People who live in glass houses should make sure to pull the blinds while removing their trousers. —Spike Milligan

143. Basketball is the second most exciting indoor sport, and the other one shouldn't have spectators. —Dick Vertleib

144. Sex? Unfortunately, as you get older, there are other things that become more important in your daily life. —Alex Trebek

145. I stopped getting the girl about ten years ago, which is just as well because I'd forgotten what I wanted her for. —John Wayne

146. There is only one remark to which there is no answer: "What are you doing with my wife?" —Miguel de Cervantes

147. Shopping is better than sex. If you're not satisfied, you can make an exchange for something you really like. —Adrienne Gusoff

148. While performing onstage I am making love to twenty-five thousand people. And then I go home alone. —Janis Joplin

149. No one in their right mind would call me a nymphomaniac. After all, I only sleep with good-looking men. —Fiona Pitt-Kethley

150. Just give me golf clubs, fresh air, and a beautiful partner, and you can keep the golf clubs and fresh air. —Jack Benny

151. I heard guys say they got into rock and roll to pick up women. I didn't get into rock to pick up women, but I sure adapted. —Ted Nugent

152. Teenage boys who have sex with their hot blonde teachers aren't damaged kids. They're lucky bastards. —George Carlin

153. Women might be capable of faking orgasm, but only men are capable of faking whole relationships. —Sharon Stone

154. The secret to long life is yoga, physical exercise, eating well, and sex. Lots of sex. As much sex as you can get. —Cyndi Lauper

155. A kiss can be a comma, a question mark, or an exclamation point. That's basic spelling all women ought to know. —Mistinguett

156. What a man enjoys about a woman's clothes are his fantasies of how she would look without them. —Brendan Francis

157. Who would have ever thought you could die from sex? It was much more fun when you just went to hell. —John Waters

158. If I were asked for a one-line answer to "What makes a woman good in bed?" I would say, "A man who is good in bed." —Bob Guccione

Solutions

159. The last woman I had sex with absolutely hated me. I could tell by the way she asked for the money. —Drew Carey

160. We have reason to believe that man first walked upright to free his hands for masturbation. —Lily Tomlin

161. A bikini is just like a barbed-wire fence. It manages to protect the property without obstructing the view. —Joey Adams

162. Anyone who eats three meals a day should understand why cookbooks outsell sex books three to one. —L.M. Boyd

163. What men call gallantry and gods call adultery is much more common where the climate is sultry. —Lord Byron

164. Men really talk to women just so they can sleep with them and women sleep with men just so they can talk to them. —Jay McInerney

165. My mother-in-law broke up my marriage. One day my wife came home early from work and found us in bed together. —Lenny Bruce

166. Man will go to any length for sexual intercourse. He will risk fortune, character, reputation—life itself. —Mark Twain

167. I've slept only with men I've been married to. How many women can honestly state that claim? —Elizabeth Taylor

168. The lovely thing about being forty is that you can appreciate twenty-five-year-old men more. —Colleen McCullough

169. We think about sex obsessively except during the physical act, when our minds begin to wander. —Howard Nemerov

170. On the topic of faked orgasms, if sex fraud were a crime, most women would go to prison the rest of their lives. —Merrill Markoe

171. The big difference between sex for money and sex for free is that sex for money usually costs a lot less. —Brendan Behan

172. I think the perfect lover is someone who turns into a pizza at four o'clock in the morning. —Charles Pierce

173. I wanted to be a priest, but when they told me I could never have sex—not even on my birthday—I changed my mind. —Johnny Vegas

174. If you are living with a man, you don't have to worry about whether you should sleep with him after dinner. —Stephanie Brush

175. Really, that little dealybob is much too far from the hole. It should really be built right in. —Loretta Lynn

176. I'm lucky that I'm not bisexual. I don't think I could stand being rejected by men as well as women. —Bernard Manning

177. Accept every blind date you can get, even with a girl who wears jeans. Maybe you can talk her out of them. —Abigail Van Buren

178. Half the women in this country can't orgasm. If it were the males, it would be declared a national emergency. —Margo St. James

179. Sex was designed to be short, nasty, and brutish. If what you want is cuddling, you should buy a puppy. —Julie Burchill

180. Vacuuming carpets, reading novels, and eating chocolate are only ways of passing time until you can fuck again. —Cynthia Heimel

181. Gentlemen don't prefer blondes. I think if I were writing that book today, I'd call it "Gentlemen Prefer Gentlemen." —Anita Loos

182. I am constantly amazed when I talk to young people to learn how much they know about sex and how little about soap. —Billie Burke

183. A hundred years ago Hester Prynne was given an A for Adultery. Today she would score no better than a C-plus. —Peter De Vries

184. Sex is great, but it's never as great as it was when you were a child, when it was still all a big mystery. —David Duchovny

185. If you're lucky enough to sleep with a pretty girl, make that your secret. The best way to ruin it is to tell people about it. —Rip Torn

186. It doesn't matter where you hide your sex magazines because your teenager will make sure to find them. —Bruce Lansky

187. What is a kiss, actually? A rosy dot over the "I" of "loving." A secret told to the mouth instead of the ear. —Edmond Rostand

188. I once had dinner with Madonna. I wasn't nervous, but within about a minute I found myself talking about underwear. —Randy Newman

189. Sending your girl's love letters to your rival after he has married her is one effective form of revenge. —Ambrose Bierce

190. It sounds strange for me to be saying this, but I've come to the conclusion that sex really is for procreation. —Eric Clapton

191. I am in favor of obeying the French habit of kissing ladies' hands. After all, one must start somewhere. —Sacha Guitry

192. A woman tries her best to get all she can out of a man, and a man tries his best to get all he can into a woman. —Isaac Goldberg

193. If you really want to look sexy in a photo, you'd better be thinking about sex rather than about being sexy. —Peta Wilson

194. It is a sign of a dull nature to be overoccupied about exercise, eating and drinking, or sexual intercourse. —Epictetus

195. An intellectual is somebody who has found something more interesting to talk about than sex. —Aldous Huxley

196. If you resolve to give up smoking, drinking, and loving, you don't actually live longer; it just seems longer. —Clement Freud

197. Literature is mostly about sex and not much about having children while life is the other way around. —David Lodge

198. When the grandmothers of today's world hear the word "Chippendales," they no longer just think of the chairs. —Jean Kerr

199. Thunder and lightning might actually be nothing more than crazy sex between Heaven and Earth. —Leonid S. Sukhorukov

200. There is nothing that compares to a kiss long and hot down to your soul that almost paralyzes you. —James Joyce

201. People's attitudes about sex aren't healthy anywhere, except maybe in those tribes where they go around naked. —Asia Argento

202. Any businessman would be foolish to fool around with his secretary. If it's somebody else's secretary, go ahead. —Barry Goldwater

203. Be careful. If you use an electric vibrator near water, you will come and go at the same time. —Louise Sammons

204. When he's late for dinner, he's either having an affair or is lying dead in the street. I always hope it's the street. —Jessica Tandy

205. It is one of the superstitions of the human mind to have imagined that virginity could be a virtue. —Voltaire

206. Kissing is a means of getting two people so close together that they can't see anything wrong with each other. —Rene Yasenek

207. Women are a problem, but if you haven't already guessed, they are the kind of problem I enjoy wrestling with. —Warren Beatty

208. I have a bronze statue of myself, naked. I have these really big curls and water comes out of every curl. It's hot. —Macy Gray

209. If all the girls attending the Yale prom were laid end to end, it wouldn't at all surprise me. —Dorothy Parker

210. In Hollywood, a starlet is what people call any woman under thirty who is not actively employed in a brothel. —Ben Hecht

211. Sentimentality gets in the way of life; how many times have we gone out looking for sex and found only love? —French Wall

212. Everything about phone sex is wonderful. Except for the part where we fight over who gets to be the receiver. —Shawn Kennedy

213. There goes an old saying, and 'twas shrewdly said, "Old fish at the table, but young flesh in bed." —Alexander Pope

214. Man's naked form is timeless and eternal and can be looked upon with joy by people of all ages. —Auguste Rodin

215. Tell me what a man finds sexually attractive and I will tell you his entire philosophy of life. —Ayn Rand

216. It's liberating to be naked in front of a hundred people, but there's nothing sexual about lovemaking on a movie set. —Bill Paxton

217. All dresses are merely variations on the eternal struggle between desire to dress and the desire to be undressed. —Lin Yutang

218. What's known as sex drive is nothing more than the motor memory of previously experienced pleasure. —William Reich

219. These men who go around explaining how they write poems ... it's like explaining how you sleep with your wife. —Philip Larkin

220. It's a universally held opinion that every woman is only two drinks away from a girl-on-girl adventure. —David Spade

221. I don't care. I've got hormones and sex is there, so why not? Sex is good. Everybody does it, and everybody should. —Robbie Williams

222. I'm the person most likely to sleep with my female fans. I just genuinely love other women. They know that. —Angelina Jolie

223. Sex is perhaps like culture: a luxury that only becomes an art after generations of leisurely acceptance. —Alice B. Toklas

224. People assume to play a sexually open character like Samantha, I must have had fabulous sex for most of my life. —Kim Cattrall

225. The title "Kiss Kiss Bang Bang" is perhaps the briefest summary possible of the basic appeal of movies. —Pauline Kael

226. Our director joked that two men herding sheep was way more sexual than two men having sex on screen. —Jake Gyllenhaal

227. It's ill-becoming for an old broad to sing about how bad she wants it, but occasionally we do anyway. —Lena Horne

228. You need a sense of humor about sex, because when you look at it, it's all somewhat ridiculous, isn't it? —Cat Deeley

229. What's the difference between a whore and a congressman? A congressman makes more money. —Edward Abbey

230. If sensuality were happiness, beasts were happier than men; but human felicity is lodged in the soul, not in the flesh. —Seneca

231. Don't you find it interesting how the sounds are the same for an awful nightmare and great sex? —Rue McClanahan

232. The primary function of muscle is to pull and not to push, except in the case of the genitals and the tongue. —Leonardo da Vinci

233. In lovemaking, as in the other arts, those do it best who cannot tell how it is done. —James M. Barrie

234. I'm so unlucky with women that if I was to fall into a barrel of nipples, I'd come out sucking my thumb. —Freddie Starr

235. The kiss is a wordless articulation of desire whose object lies in the future, and somewhat to the south. —Lance Morrow

236. I can make love for eight hours. But this includes four hours of begging followed by dinner and a movie. —Sting

237. Acting is easy. If I have to cry, I just think of my sex life, and if I have to laugh, I just think of my sex life. —Glenda Jackson

238. Make love to every broad you meet. If you get five percent on your outlay, consider it a good investment. —Arnold Bennett

239. My cousin is an agoraphobic homosexual, which makes it kind of hard for him to come out of the closet. —Bill Kelly

240. I believe that sex is one of the most beautiful, natural, wholesome things that money can buy. —Steve Martin

241. A rose was once named after me, but the catalog description read: no good in bed, but fine up against a wall. —Eleanor Roosevelt

242. Everyone shows their thong out the back of their jeans. You'll get a much better line if you wear no knickers. —Victoria Beckham

243. Cricket is the greatest pastime God created. Certainly much better than sex, although sex isn't too bad either. —Harold Pinter

244. Statistics are like a bikini: what they reveal is suggestive but what they conceal is vital. —Aaron Levenstein

245. Fidelity is possible. Anything is possible if you're stubborn and strong. But it's not that important. —Michelle Pfeiffer

246. I have a tattoo on my most private part of Mickey and Minnie Mouse involved in a sex act. It's my sense of humor. —Janet Jackson

Solutions

247. You cannot blame pornography. When I was a young child, I used to masturbate to "Gilligan's Island." —Ron Jeremy

248. The only interesting thing that can happen in a Swiss bedroom is suffocation by a feather mattress. —Dalton Trumbo

249. I like feet. I definitely have a fetish. I love to see a man's bare foot, but it's got to be nicely manicured. —Brooke Burke

250. Social progress can be marked exactly by the social position of the fair sex—the ugly ones included. —Karl Marx

251. Latins are tenderly enthusiastic. In Brazil they throw flowers at you. In Argentina they throw themselves. —Marlene Dietrich

252. I support the theory that anyone can get laid. It's simply a matter of lowering your standards enough. —Michael Stipe

253. Sexual passion is largely an emotion of power and domination. Nothing says, "Mine, mine" more fiercely. —Charles Horton Cooley

254. I was a prostitute for months before it hit me. I liked it so much, I couldn't imagine it was prostitution. —Annie Sprinkle

255. Sex is the Tabasco sauce which an adolescent national palate sprinkles on every course in the menu. —Mary Day Winn

256. Three words you would probably rather not hear while you're busy making love are, "Honey! I'm home!" —Ken Hammond

257. The modern theory is that you can have both love and sex in a marriage; no previous society believed this. —Alain de Botton

258. My most memorable partner is always the present one; the rest all merge into a sea of blondes. —Rod Stewart

259. My wife doesn't care what I do while I'm away from home as long as I don't have a good time while I'm doing it. —Lee Trevino

260. "Where should one use perfume?" a woman once asked me. "Wherever one wants to be kissed," I replied. —Coco Chanel

261. Homosexuality is God's way of insuring that the truly gifted aren't burdened with children. —Sam Austin

262. My advice to you is not to inquire why or whither, but to just enjoy your ice cream while it is on your plate. —Thornton Wilder

263. Republicans sleep in twin beds—some even in separate rooms. That is why there are more Democrats. —Will Stanton

264. Sure we all worry about the population explosion, but we never worry about it at the right time. —Arthur Hoppe

265. I think it's cool to have sex with someone when you're not supposed to. It's cool to be sneaky about it. —Carmen Electra

266. Flesh sells. People don't want to see pictures of churches. They want to see naked bodies. —Helen Mirren

267. B is for breasts, of which ladies have two; once prized for the function, now for the view. —Robert Paul Smith

268. You can't beat sex outdoors. I like forests, barns, swimming pool changing rooms, on top of hills, you name it. —Katie Price

269. I've got great cleavage, great hair, and great legs. I make certain those bits are what people's eyes are drawn to. —Barbara Atkin

270. The sign of a true crush is that you fall in love with each other first and grope for reasons afterward. —Shana Alexander

271. No one can sleep with Dick. He wakes up during the night, switches on the lights, and speaks into his tape recorder. —Pat Nixon

272. Never become sexually involved with anyone you genuinely care about. A sexual relationship guarantees a loss. —Mary Gordon

273. Passion develops quickly and is quickest to fade. Intimacy develops slowly, and commitment more gradually still. —Robert Sternberg

274. The lovebird will be one hundred percent faithful to his mate as long as they're locked together in the same cage. —Will Cuppy

275. I can picture two guys because there is something to grab hold of. But how do two insides make love? —Lydia Lopokova

276. Erection is chiefly caused by parsnips, artichokes, turnips, asparagus, candied ginger, and so forth. —Aristotle

277. TV advertising is just like sex and taxes; the more talk there is about them, the less likely they are to be curbed. —Jack Gould

278. Girls who are having a good sex thing stay in New York. The rest want to spend their summer vacations in Europe. —Gail Parent

279. I like being outdoors. I like to skip in the forests in the nude. It is another world to take sunbaths in the nude. —Bettie Page

280. A woman may have a cleaner mind than a man, but that's only because she changes hers more often. —Oliver Herford

281. When somebody gives you a sexy look, you know they're trying. But when you smile, it's so much sexier. —Carol Alt

282. Safe sex—with a condom, rubber gloves, and a wetsuit—is perfectly okay as long as you don't fall in love. —Kerry Thornley

283. The thing I like most about celibacy is that you don't need to bother reading the manual. —Sheldon Keller

284. The only reason that I would take up jogging is so that I could hear heavy breathing again. —Erma Bombeck

285. How did sex come to be thought of as dirty in the first place? God must have been a Republican. —Will Durst

286. A man can have two, maybe three love affairs while he's married. But after that, it's cheating. —Yves Montand

287. Golf and sex are probably the only two things you can enjoy without actually being any good at them. —Jimmy Demaret

288. The fantasy of every Australian man is to have two women—one cleaning and the other dusting. —Maureen Murphy

289. They tell me, "Okay, this is where we're going to push up your cleavage," and I'm like, "What cleavage?" —Natalie Portman

290. Whenever I hear people discussing birth control, I always remember that I was the fifth child. —Clarence Darrow

Solutions

291. All really great lovers are articulate, and verbal seduction is the surest road to actual seduction. —Marya Mannes

292. Nuptial love maketh mankind; friendly love perfecteth it; but wanton love corrupteth and embaseth it. —Francis Bacon

293. Kiss, remain active, enjoy it, talk dirty, be encouraging, and don't say stupid things like, "Are you done yet?" —Spry Magazine

294. Of all the worldly passions, lust is the most intense. All other worldly passions seem to follow in its train. —Buddha

295. Sex education may be a good idea in the schools, but I don't believe the kids should be given homework. —Bill Cosby

296. Vibrators? I think they are great. They keep you out of stupid sex. I'd recommend them to everybody. —Anne Heche

297. I'm a pretty open person. Like when I have good sex, the next day I'm going to tell everyone I know. —Melissa Joan Hart

298. Married sex is like being awake during your own autopsy. It is root canal work without anesthetic. —Al Goldstein

299. Sex isn't the primary element of the universe. It's just that when it's unfulfilled, it will affect you. —Jack Nicholson

300. I am going to my room to masturbate before I have a light lunch, if you would like to come and watch. —Salvador Dalí

301. Men are very goal-oriented. They believe in the hereafter. An orgasm is what they are here after. —Alan Altman

302. If you want great sex, find a partner who really turns you on. Pills are just props, and props are a drag. —Jackie Collins

303. I wouldn't propose sex, drugs, or insanity for everybody, but they've always worked for me. —Hunter S. Thompson

304. One of the advantages of living alone is that you don't have to wake up in the arms of a loved one. —Marion Smith

305. I can't be with somebody just because it's great sex, because orgasms don't last long enough. —Courtney Cox

306. We always make it a point to practice safe sex. We gave up the chandelier a very long time ago. —Kathie Lee Gifford

307. Girls are much more psychic than guys. They're the first to know if you're going to get laid. —Paul Rodriguez

308. I know the ways of women; they won't come when thou wilt, and when thou won't they are passionately fond. —Terence

309. A man who exposes himself while he is intoxicated appreciates not the art of getting drunk. —Samuel Johnson

310. If goodness is its own reward, then couldn't we get a little something for being naughty? —Lauren Bacall

311. A couple engaged in a sexual experience is happy for that moment. Then very soon trouble begins. —The Dalai Lama

312. Well, since I've never watched anybody make love before, how do you know if you're doing it right? —Kevin Costner

313. Anybody who thinks that the way to a man's heart is through his stomach flunked geography. —Robert Byrne

314. Very simply, a promiscuous person is anyone who is getting more sex than you are. —Victor Lownes

315. I never expected to see the day when girls would get sunburned in the places they do today. —Will Rogers

316. It is with our passions, as it is with fire and water, that they form good servants but bad masters. —Aesop

317. Sex: the pleasure is momentary, the position ridiculous, and the expense damnable. —Lord Chesterfield

318. A man loses his sense of direction after four drinks; a woman loses hers after four kisses. —H.L. Mencken

319. If I've still got my pants on during the second scene, I figure they've sent me the wrong script. —Mel Gibson

320. I came to America in pursuit of my lifelong quest for naked women in wet mackintoshes. —Dylan Thomas

321. There is a special place you can touch a woman that will drive her crazy. Her heart. —Melanie Griffith

322. My dad told me, "Anything worth doing is worth waiting for." I waited until I was fifteen. —Zsa Zsa Gabor

323. How could a woman look at an erect penis without going off into mad gales of laughter? —Stephen King

324. Nothing men do surprises me anymore. I'm ready for them. I know how to whack below the belt. —Patsy Cline

325. How well a soft and libertine voice will erect your member, for it is just as good as fingers. —Juvenal

326. Sex is more exciting on the screen and between the pages than it is between the sheets. —Andy Warhol

327. Condoms aren't completely safe. A friend of mine was wearing one when he got hit by a bus. —Bob Rubin

328. The most romantic line any woman ever said to me in bed was, "Are you sure you're not a cop?" —Larry Brown

329. One of the nicest things about masturbation is that you don't have to dress up for it. —Truman Capote

330. Yes, men crave sex, that's how we are. It's why the penis is shaped like a compass needle. —Peter MacNicol

331. My town was so small that they taught everyone driver's ed and sex ed in the same car. —Mary Sue Terry

332. The troubling thing about my wife is that she's a whore in the kitchen and a cook in bed. —Geoffrey Gorer

333. When my girl is sober, she pleases me a little, but when she is drunk, she delights me. —Propertius

334. To the Latin, sex is just an hors d'oeuvre; to the Anglo-Saxon, sex is a barbecue. —George Jean Nathan

335. I'm a sex machine for both genders. It's all very exhausting. I need a lot of sleep. —Rupert Everett

336. It's the good girls that keep the diaries; the bad girls never have the time. —Tallulah Bankhead

337. My husband is German. Every night I dress up like Poland and let him invade me. —Bette Midler

338. Love is just a system for getting somebody to call you darling after sex. —Julian Barnes

339. I'm not against half-naked girls. At least not nearly as often as I'd like to be. —Benny Hill

340. Good men keep dogs but order them to leave the room during lovemaking. —Erika Ritter

Hints

Threesome #1	Threesome #8	Threesome #15	19. F→S	53. R→T
1. P→L	1. F→N	1. E→T	20. O→H	54. V→A
2. O→N	2. R→E	2. A→D	21. Z→L	55. U→A
3. G→T	3. K→T	3. W→R	22. X→T	56. K→N
			23. X→I	57. L→R
Threesome #2	Threesome #9	Threesome #16	24. T→G	58. C→M
1. Y→E	1. Y→D	1. W→A	25. B→O	59. D→I
2. P→A	2. I→T	2. J→E	26. G→N	60. X→A
3. J→R	3. X→H	3. V→I	27. O→A	61. G→U
			28. O→D	62. M→L
Threesome #3	Threesome #10	Threesome #17	29. J→O	63. Z→T
1. M→E	1. V→S	1. B→N	30. Y→O	64. L→G
2. J→A	2. M→G	2. Z→T	31. B→Y	65. B→S
3. C→T	3. F→S	3. Q→T	32. B→U	66. B→Y
			33. I→O	67. D→B
Threesome #4	Threesome #11	Nice and Long	34. M→E	68. I→N
1. W→G	1. K→H	1. V→A	35. Q→W	69. G→O
2. G→I	2. Q→B	2. J→O	36. J→A	70. H→T
3. A→N	3. Y→O	3. R→T	37. W→L	71. O→I
		4. R→N	38. D→I	72. L→A
Threesome #5	Threesome #12	5. C→R	39. L→T	73. D→T
1. C→T	1. I→N	6. V→Y	40. N→R	74. B→C
2. A→L	2. S→H	7. J→W	41. X→N	75. A→W
3. U→E	3. Z→E	8. X→S	42. D→A	76. U→R
		9. Y→L	43. V→S	77. G→S
Threesome #6	Threesome #13	10. D→H	44. C→I	78. L→O
1. Q→N	1. D→N	11. G→O	45. L→O	79. J→D
2. Q→H	2. X→T	12. M→C	46. K→C	80. O→U
3. C→O	3. S→M	13. E→T	47. O→N	81. O→L
		14. J→N	48. J→S	82. S→W
Threesome #7	Threesome #14	15. W→M	49. N→M	83. X→N
1. A→M	1. B→O	16. M→A	50. L→H	84. E→Y
2. S→O	2. K→T	17. Q→D	51. N→L	85. Z→I
3. L→N	3. I→S	18. G→E	52. K→O	86. B→A

Harder, Harder
87. A→E
88. K→N
89. I→S
90. F→Y
91. B→I
92. A→O
93. Z→E
94. S→B
95. X→M
96. F→S
97. I→L
98. X→U
99. Y→A
100. U→O
101. A→L
102. O→N
103. H→R
104. X→N
105. T→D
106. T→A
107. P→S
108. A→T
109. B→N
110. W→O
111. K→S
112. R→N
113. E→H
114. R→A
115. R→E
116. D→L
117. N→I
118. L→O
119. X→A
120. V→O
121. S→T
122. O→W
123. G→N
124. O→E
125. J→I
126. C→E
127. P→Y
128. H→S
129. X→H
130. H→D
131. T→N
132. T→W
133. E→D
134. Y→O
135. M→R
136. P→I
137. R→A

138. U→E
139. Z→T
140. R→L
141. N→H
142. Z→O
143. X→O
144. J→A
145. V→G
146. Q→R
147. A→T
148. R→A
149. N→T
150. K→U
151. T→I
152. L→H
153. U→E
154. X→C
155. K→M
156. D→T
157. H→W
158. Z→N
159. I→L
160. R→I
161. C→A
162. Z→S
163. Q→M
164. P→T
165. J→O
166. X→R
167. P→N
168. V→L
169. U→O
170. H→T
171. T→A
172. N→C
173. D→Y
174. V→R
175. J→E
176. C→E
177. L→N
178. B→M
179. R→T
180. Y→I
181. F→O
182. Y→L
183. T→S
184. I→W
185. G→P
186. N→A
187. I→E
188. G→U
189. E→O

190. V→R
191. L→H
192. O→N
193. W→B
194. X→U
195. P→S
196. S→O
197. N→A
198. Q→D
199. R→H
200. V→A
201. S→N
202. P→L
203. C→A
204. K→R
205. E→N
206. N→G
207. J→R
208. L→O
209. F→R
210. K→L
211. L→T
212. J→O
213. V→S
214. G→D
215. U→E
216. V→U
217. C→N
218. S→A
219. X→H
220. D→N
221. T→R
222. O→I
223. H→C
224. B→O
225. L→P
226. G→W
227. T→B
228. C→O
229. X→N
230. O→L
231. J→U
232. Q→C
233. T→S
234. J→N
235. N→I
236. C→G
237. M→E
238. Y→R
239. Y→C
240. P→S
241. X→D

242. C→I
243. G→I
244. B→S
245. J→N
246. Y→M
247. O→T
248. C→O
249. H→F
250. A→C
251. U→N
252. G→R
253. S→M
254. Q→E
255. L→I
256. O→H
257. P→N
258. Y→O
259. C→W
260. M→O
261. Q→N
262. P→Y
263. M→N
264. P→U
265. I→N
266. A→T
267. P→I
268. O→E
269. F→R
270. K→F
271. C→S
272. Y→L
273. K→A
274. E→R
275. X→E
276. L→E
277. C→L
278. P→G
279. Q→N
280. N→M
281. M→Y
282. Q→D
283. K→A
284. H→G
285. D→T
286. L→N
287. X→Y
288. Q→O
289. Z→G
290. N→W
291. M→C
292. M→I
293. N→Y

294. M→E
295. S→T
296. J→Y
297. L→G
298. N→W
299. W→F
300. D→L
301. K→H
302. F→D
303. Q→R
304. K→V
305. D→U
306. X→O
307. B→G
308. P→Y
309. R→S

For Sexperts Only
310. H→E
311. S→N
312. C→R
313. M→O
314. G→I
315. Y→D
316. A→E
317. E→A
318. F→R
319. U→S
320. K→N
321. X→I
322. K→A
323. W→E
324. Q→H
325. X→S
326. E→S
327. D→A
328. V→R
329. Q→O
330. Q→S
331. C→Y
332. X→N
333. O→H
334. N→S
335. U→T
336. Q→I
337. E→D
338. B→E
339. Q→A
340. V→E

Hints